Constructing TELEVISION

Sue & Wink Hackman

HODDER AND STOUGHTON
LONDON SYDNEY AUCKLAND TORONTO

British Library Cataloguing in Publication Data

Hackman, Sue
 Constructing television.
 1. Great Britain. Television programmes.
 Production
 I. Title II. Hackman, Wink
 791.45'0232'0941

 ISBN 0-340-49323-2

First published 1989

Copyright © 1989 Sue and Wink Hackman

All rights reserved. Except as specified on p. 5, no part of this publication may be reproduced or transmitted in any form or by any means, electronically or mechanically, including photocopying, recording or any information storage or retrieval system, without permission in writing from the publisher or under licence from the Copyright Licensing Agency Limited. Details of such licences (for reprographic reproduction) may be obtained from the Copyright Licensing Agency Limited of 33–34 Alfred Place, London WC1E 7DP.

Typeset by Wearside Tradespools, Fulwell, Sunderland

Printed and bound in Great Britain for Hodder and Stoughton Educational, a division of Hodder and Stoughton Ltd, Mill Road, Dunton Green, Sevenoaks, Kent by Butler & Tanner Ltd, Frome and London

Contents

Acknowledgments 4

Note to the Teacher 5

Preface 6

PART ONE: JUST LIKE LIFE? 7

Making a Drama Programme 8
Imaginary Worlds 10
Storytelling 21
Stories 26
The Craft of Fiction 31
Special Project: Five-Minute Theatre 41

PART TWO: FACING THE FACTS 43

A News Story in the Making 44
Reporting the News 47
News as Narrative 55
Newsworthiness 65
News Appeal 77
Working with Rushes 80
Special Project: Local News Bulletin 82

PART THREE: THE ART OF PERSUASION 87

Making a Television Advertisement 88
Making a Market 91
Creating Consumers 99
Talking Pictures 103
The Language of Persuasion 107
Special Project: School for Sale 115

PART FOUR: A POINT OF VIEW 119

Making a Video in the Community 120
Taming the Medium 123
Try it Yourself 128
Making the Most of It 134
Reclaiming the Image 138
Special Project: Video Dispatch 141

Acknowledgments

The authors and publishers would like to thank the following for permission to reproduce material in this book:

Korda Films/Central Independent Television for the film still from *The Shape of Things to Come* on p. 12; Secker & Warburg Ltd for the photograph from *In Flagrante* by Chris Killip on pp. 47 and 54; BBC Hulton Picture Library for the photographs on pp. 48 and 54; Topham Picture Library for the photographs on pp. 51, 55, 64, 74, 107; ITN for the transcript on p. 73; Oxfam for the photographs on pp. 78–9; Midland Bank/Allen, Brady and Marsh for the transcript and still from the Orchard advertisement on p. 95; John Harvey and Sons Ltd for the advertisement on p. 99; The Mortgage Corporation/McCarthy, Cosby and Paul Ltd/Bruce Fleming for the top right photograph on p. 106; J. Walter Thompson Company/Elida Gibbs Limited for the transcript of the Timotei advertisement on p. 108; Van den Berghs and Jurgens Limited for the transcript of the Latta advertisement on p. 109; Coca-Cola Great Britain for the song and logo on p. 110 (Coca-Cola and Coke are registered trademarks which identify the same product of The Coca-Cola Company); Maxwell House/D'arcy, Masius, Benton and Bowles for the transcript of the advertisement on p. 110; Nationwide Anglia/Leagas and Delaney for the transcript of the advertisement on p. 111; Vauxhall/Lowe, Howard and Spink for the transcripts of the advertisements on pp. 112–113; Business Television Ltd for the transcript from *Business Daily* on pp. 113–14; Tony Lavender for the extracts from the Scottish Television booklet *Time to Think* on pp. 129, 130, 131, 132, 133; Universal Pictorial Press and Agency Ltd for the photograph on p. 138.

Note to the Teacher

This book accompanies four programmes made by Scottish Television entitled *Constructing Television*, made as part of the *Time to Think* series. Each of our chapters takes up the themes initiated by these programmes. Although the book is designed for independent use, teachers who have copies of the programmes will find that all the chapters draw on them for exemplar material, quotations from production staff and exercise material. In particular, we are indebted to Scottish Television for the photographic illustrations in this book, most of which are culled from the *Time to Think* programmes.

The introductory sections to the chapters act as résumés of the programmes and we recommend teachers to use the recorded videos with their classes. A viewing of the production process in action is more eloquent than any description.

The special projects which conclude each section are full-day practical assignments which offer students firsthand experience of the pressures, constraints and pleasures of video production. Detailed information about the management of these sessions can be found in the 'Try it Yourself' section on p. 128. Addressed to students, this section offers guidance about planning, organisation, procedure and assessment, as well as practical advice.

Recorded videotapes of the four programmes can be obtained from the publishers at the following address:

> Hodder and Stoughton
> Special Order Department
> Dunton Green
> Sevenoaks
> Kent TN13 1YY.

In addition, a special tape of outtakes from the news report of the Glasgow health workers' demonstration studied in 'Facing The Facts' can be obtained from:

> Scottish Television plc
> Programme Sales
> Cowcaddens
> Glasgow G2 3PR.

Pages 35, 47, 74–5, 108, 109, 133, 134, 135 may be photocopied for class use only.

Preface

Television has been with us now for over 50 years. The students we teach have grown up with it. To ignore television is to disregard the increasing sophistication of its output and the massive following it has amongst students of all ages and abilities. The study of television is a truly mixed-ability enterprise to which students bring a rich and ready fund of knowledge and expertise.

The four sections of *Constructing Television* represent key areas for intensive study. At the time of writing, over 35 per cent of peaktime television programming is fiction. The first section, 'Just Like Life?', looks at television drama and the production processes which lie behind it. We may well consider *Great Expectations* a better cultural experience than *EastEnders*, but it is television which shapes and feeds the fictional imaginations of our students. For most of them, television is also their primary source of news. Teachers need to be alert to the fallacy that factual programmes offer a transparent window on the world. It is in the second section, 'Facing the Facts', that we explore the way production decisions give ideological shape to the news. We deal with advertising in the third section, 'The Art Of Persuasion', in the knowledge that many students enjoy the commercials as much as the programmes – and sometimes more so. Commercials, with their generous budgets and compact format, have an appealing directness and ingenuity. They are often in the vanguard of televisual innovation, and deserve more than a casual dismissal. A quarter of this book is devoted to community video. For most people, school provides their only opportunity to gain hands-on experience in video. In the fourth section, 'A Point of View', and also in the practical exercises, we aim to build students' confidence, experience and understanding of television production.

Seeing the production process at work leads us to appreciate the way programme ideology is generated by working practices, practical constraints and production decisions. In this respect, we would refer readers to the Scottish Television series *Time to Think*, with which this book is linked and of which there is a video cassette (comprising the four programmes in the series) available from the publishers. We would like to thank Scottish Television for the time and help they gave us while producing this book and in particular, David Butts (the writer of the series), Iain Morris (the programme editor) and Mary Magowan (the editorial assistant).

Sue and Wink Hackman

PART ONE

Just Like Life?

Making a Drama Programme

Television drama is created by a team of people whose jobs range from scriptwriting to set construction. Some of these people work full-time for the television companies, and others work freelance. A successful programme may return for several series, involving years of continuing work. This is true of *Taggart*, a popular detective series made by Scottish Television.

Robert Love is the executive producer of *Taggart*. He bears overall responsibility for the programme, organising staff and resources to bring it from an idea to the screen. His starting point is to discuss stories and script possibilities with a scriptwriter.

The scriptwriter in this case is Glenn Chandler. He works ideas into detailed scripts. Some ideas sound good but won't work on screen. Other ideas will work, but have been done before. An experienced scriptwriter knows what will work, has an eye for originality and writes within the constraints of the available time and budget.

Actors read through the scenes, guided by the director. It is his role to interpret the script for the actors and cameras. Later, when the scene is recorded in the studio, a floor manager conveys instructions to the people at work on the studio floor while the director observes the action as seen through the cameras.

JUST LIKE LIFE?

By now, the locations manager has chosen suitable sites for the outdoor scenes. Riggers and electricians are busy assembling the equipment. The technical crew gets to work organising lighting, microphones and cameras, while the props provide the finishing touches.

Stunt artists are briefed for dangerous scenes such as this one in which a man leaps to safety from a fork-lift truck which is out of control. The stunt artist is made up to look like the original actor. Everything possible is done to minimise the risks, and to make the first 'take' the right one. If all goes well, the shoot itself is over quickly. If the scene looks wrong, or hitches occur, it must be shot again – a retake. This means time and money. At a certain point, the director must decide that the take is good enough and move on to the next.

In the editing room, the director explains how he wants to piece the scene together. The editor proceeds, shot by shot, to create a scene which is paced to hold the viewer's attention. Music and sound effects are dubbed on. They are surprisingly important in defining the atmosphere of the scene.

Imaginary Worlds

Television drama creates an imaginary world. Although the settings may look familiar and the people behave in ways we recognise, they are made up from the imagination and experience of the production team. The imaginary world is not a complete world, but one composed of fragments to give the impression of wholeness. The characters have no life outside the scenes in which they appear. Between episodes, they and their world can only exist in the creative imagination of the viewer.

Imaginary places

Here is the set for a television drama. Look closely and glean what information you can from it:

- How would you describe the atmosphere of the room?
- Where might it be?
- What year is it?
- What can you tell about the person who lives here?

Besides conveying atmosphere and information, the set must be practical. It must:

- leave room for the cameras and overhead microphone to move around
- not obstruct the camera's view
- be cheap and practical to construct

Now design a set, with props, to suit the following brief:

Set for a television comedy
Busy office in local bus depot.
Cramped, rather dilapidated.
Occupants: station manager, assistant manager and clerk/typist.
Much paperwork – schedules, letters, notices, etc.
Station manager – ruthlessly efficient and tidy but currently on leave.
Assistant manager – well-meaning but hopelessly disorganised.
Clerk typist – overworked, underpaid, fighting a losing battle against a tide of paperwork.

Many sets seem 'realistic' because they contain objects we know. But they can only be seen from certain angles; just beyond the camera's vision is the studio. If you watch your favourite soap opera or any other drama with a familiar set, you will notice that you only ever see two or three walls.

This is the set for a scene from the detective series *Taggart*:

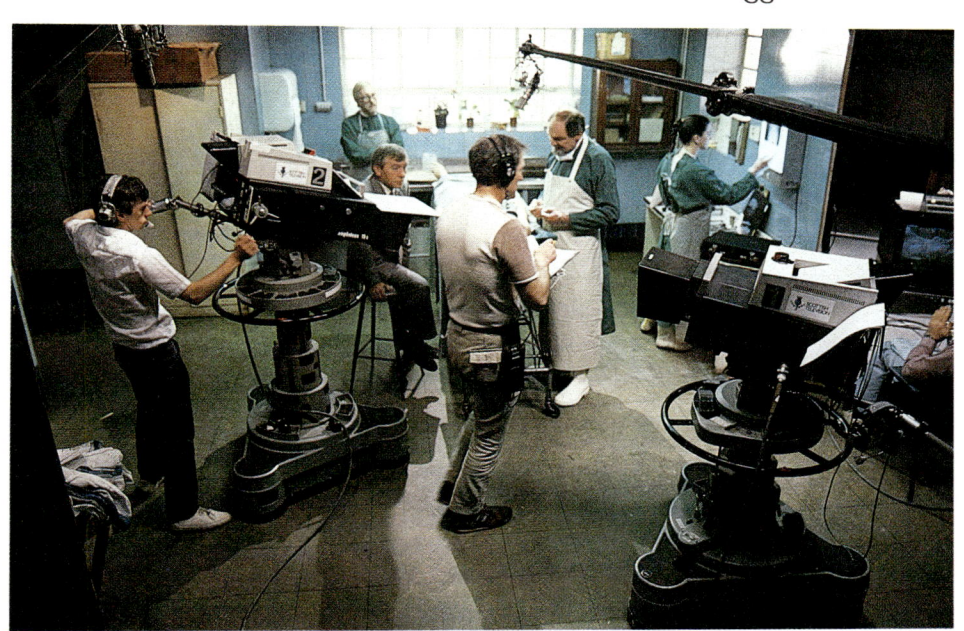

Imagine what the actors see when they look towards the imaginary fourth wall, where the cameras and technical crew are.

Dramas often include scenes set in well-known places. When we see these locations, the world of make-believe is easier to accept. *Taggart* uses Glasgow as a backdrop, building up a convincing impression of a detective working on the streets of a real city.

CONSTRUCTING TELEVISION

- What other series can you name which use familiar locations?
- In what way do the characters suit their settings?

Some sets are not meant to be familiar, but when we look back over the years, we can see that they reveal a lot about the time in which they were made.

- What date would you put on these science fiction film sets?
- What were the giveaway clues?
- Check your answers afterwards against those on page 20.
- Sum up by outlining the role of the setting in the creation of the imaginary world of drama. Explain your points by referring to sets from your favourite television programmes.

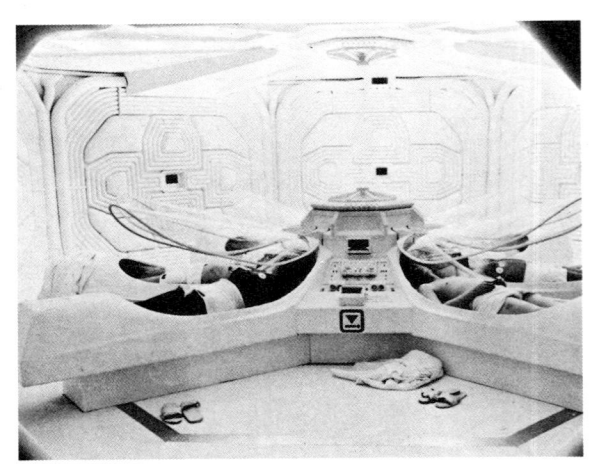

Imaginary people

Characters are created by the combined skills of the scriptwriter, actor, costume department and make-up staff. Although they have no existence outside their scenes, they may seem so lifelike that we can imagine how they would behave when we are not watching them. This illusion is the craft of characterisation – building up a complete impression of a character.

Study these character outlines:

A character in a science fiction series *The Planet People*
Name: Zealo
Residence: Garden Planet Flora
Occupation: Plant propagation adviser
Status: One of the Favoured class
Age: 2 billion mega-ticks
Family: Zealo has 15 sprouts and 12 seedlings

The Floran people are two-thirds human and one-third plant. A happy and peaceful people, they have dedicated their planet to the collection and protection of all plant life. Plants provide all their needs, including raw materials for their clothes. They eat only insects.

- Design a costume and make-up for this character.

The central character in the drama *The Bottom Line*
Name: Bill Hatchard
Residence: always on the move – hostels, floors, occasional park bench or beach
Occupation: none
Status: millionaire who has turned tramp for 12 months to see a different kind of life
Age: 45
Bill is eight months into his experiment. He carries all his possessions with him.

- Design a costume and list personal props for this character.

The appearance of a character is emphasised by the gestures, movement, and especially the speech of the actor. The scriptwriter's role here is very important. The way characters express themselves provides clues to their background and personality.

Consider these script extracts and the impression they give of the characters speaking.

(a) 'Oh Tom, darling – could I have a word? Could I ask you an enormous favour? Harvey's little nephew is doing a sponsored swim at school tomorrow afternoon and I promised to get him some names. I know it's an awful cheek, but could I put you down? Dear Quentin's ever so keen. He's been practising for weeks. . . . Charles has very kindly allowed me to put his name down for £1 a length, and it's all for charity. . . . That's very charitable. Thank you darling. Have a nice weekend. Ciao!'

(b) 'Well I've been ripped off and I ain't givin' up until I get my money back.'
    'Oh yeah, you and whose army? Look, it ain't my problem, pal, and

the best thing you can do is forget about it.'
'That's not what you said last night!'
'Yeah, well I've had a chance to sleep on it since then, and I just don't need the aggro.'

- What conclusions can you draw about the characters in each case?
- What details pointed to your conclusions?
- How fair is it to judge people by the way they speak?
- How fair is it of scriptwriters to define characters by the way they speak?

- Study these pictures and say what you can tell about the characters from their dress, make-up and stance.
- What clues led you to your conclusions?

Try communicating characters through a script. First read this outline of a scene for a television drama:

It is late. The first person is in a hurry. The other still has something on his or her mind – but is taking a lot of time saying it. Eventually, the first person has to make an exit, but just as he or she leaves, the other person comes out with it. Freeze on a shot of the first person's reaction.

- Write three versions of the script for this scene, expressed in language you find appropriate for these characters:

    – a headteacher and a student
    – two lovers
    – two rival gangsters

- Listen to each other's scripts and discuss the following points:

    – How effective are they?
    – Where do we get our ideas about the way headteachers, students, lovers and gangsters speak?
    – How trustworthy are the sources?

Running to type

The characters of television drama usually behave in predictable ways. There is not enough time in a television programme to develop characters that are as subtle and unique as real people. It is easier for the audience if they recognise a familiar type of character, so that the programme can bypass the lengthy stages of introduction. The characters have a natural air about them, but they don't often surprise us.

Here are some familiar scenarios from television drama. Read them and then decide what would **typically** happen next.

(a) Our hero is in a seemingly impossible situation. The Evil Master himself has chained him to the Laser Target Practice Board. The Laser pistol is poised to fire and the firing squad await the signal. Our hero has a matter of moments to live, unless . . .

- What does he do next?

(b) Our hero and heroine have fallen for each other. She can barely bring herself to leave his office, but is due elsewhere. His waiting-room is full. He swoops round the desk as she rises to go. Close now, face to face, they gaze deep into each other's eyes. Neither moves. Then slowly (the music starts here) they move closer . . .

- What do they do next?

(c) Our detective is parked outside the drug dealer's house when the door opens. The most wanted man in Europe steps out, jumps into a car and drives off. Our detective has orders to keep watch on the house, but . . .

- What does he do next?

(d) Our detective has followed the villain into a warehouse piled with huge crates and rows of boxes. He hears a noise and creeps to the corner of one aisle, and . . .

- What does he do next?

(e) Our young hitchhiker has been forced to take shelter in the sinister mansion of Count DeCorpus. Late at night, and unable to sleep for the howling of the storm outside, she is surprised by a sudden piercing cry from the floor below . . .

- What does she do next?

- What would *you* have done next in each case?

There are always new and amusing versions of these stock scenes, though the characters themselves are rather more conventional. A typical detective, for example, has stock characteristics.

- Which of these qualities do you most identify with the typical television detective?

  - uses intuition
  - has 'bottle'
  - is prepared to go it alone
  - is cautious
  - sticks to letter of the law
  - never ducks a confrontation
  - has a strong sense of police discipline
  - has 'a nose for the truth'
  - is impulsive
  - has respect for superiors
  - carries out painstaking research
  - always follows orders
  - never gives up on a job once started
  - is restrained
  - is conscientious about paperwork
  - is approachable
  - works well with the community
  - is reckless
  - is philosophical about defeat

Try composing a list of typical features for the following types in soap operas:

  - the gossip
  - the assertive barmaid/landlady
  - the wide boy (wheeler-dealer)

- Can you think of some other familiar types who turn up in drama?
- Discuss their common characteristics.

It is often the case that the characters in drama series operate within an enclosed society. The setting may be a street, a square, a police station or some other well-defined space. The characters know each other well and form a tightly-knit community.

- Choose the drama series you know best and draw a floorplan or map of the community, like this one of *EastEnders*' Albert Square:

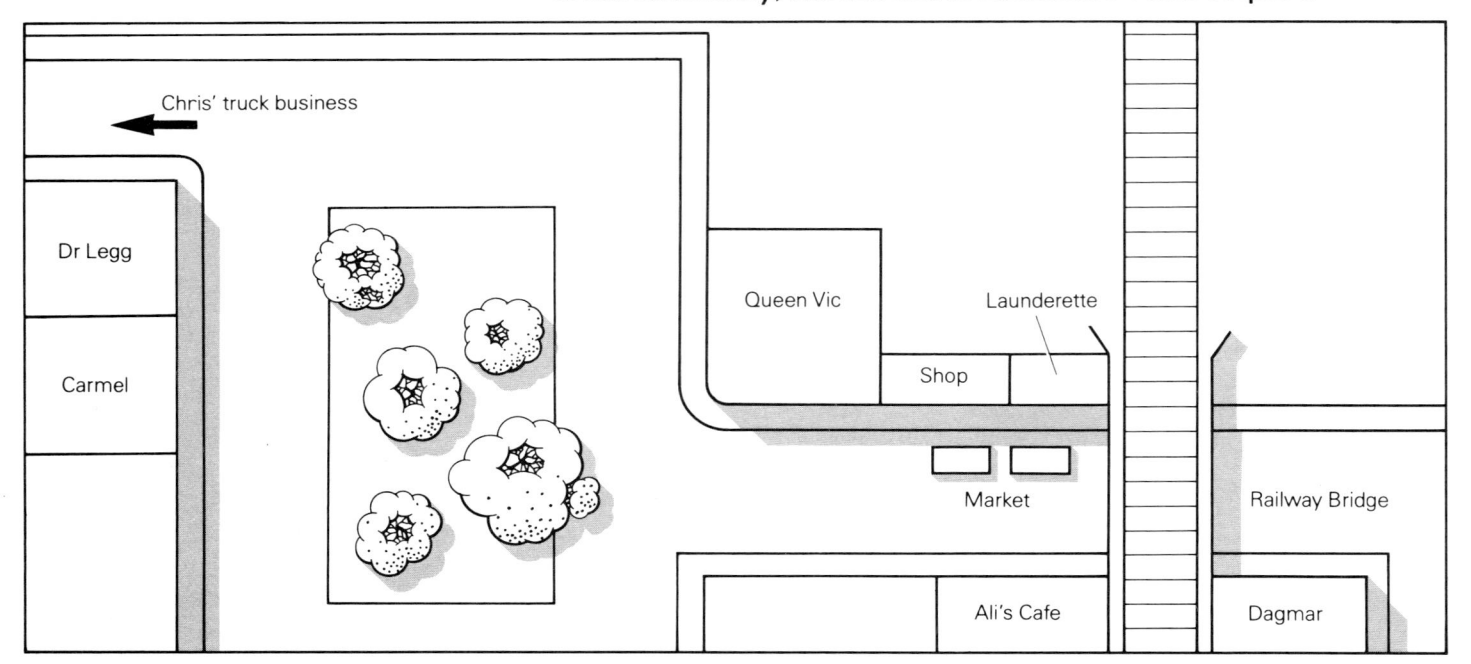

JUST LIKE LIFE?

- Familiar as we are with these communities, it is difficult to work out the layout and the distances involved. Why is this?
- Try working out a family tree or diagram to show the relationships between the characters. Notice how many and how complex the relationships are in the one shown below:

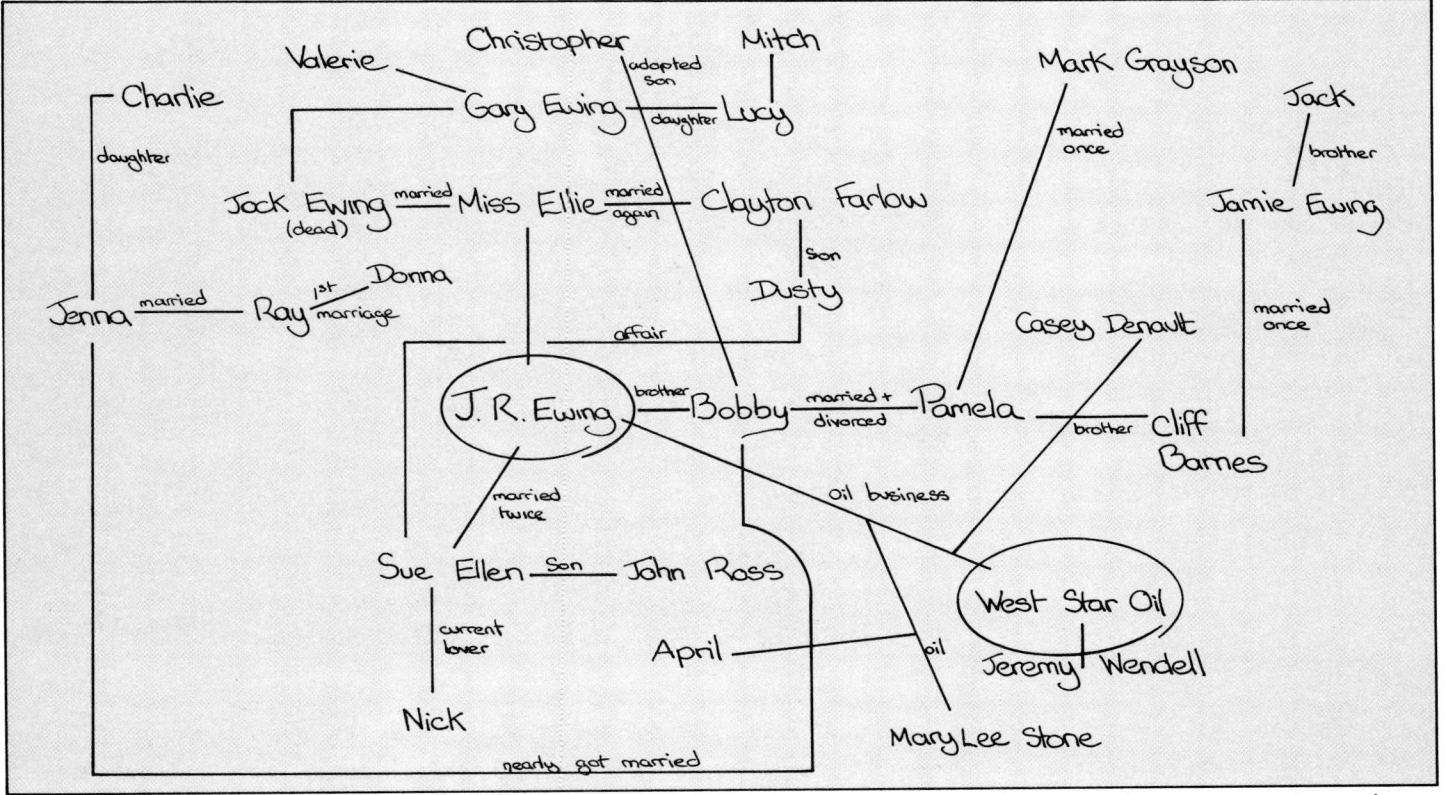

[Family tree diagram of *Dallas* characters showing: Charlie (daughter); Valerie, Christopher (adopted son), Mitch; Gary Ewing, Lucy (daughter); Jack Ewing (dead) married Miss Ellie married again Clayton Farlow; Dusty (son); Jenna married Ray (1st marriage) Donna; J.R. Ewing (married twice) — brother — Bobby married + divorced Pamela — brother — Cliff Barnes; Mark Grayson (married once); Jack (brother) Jamie Ewing (married once); Casey Denault; Sue Ellen — son — John Ross; current lover Nick; April — nearly got married; Mary Lee Stone; West Star Oil — Jeremy Wendell (oil business)]

- Why is it that so many drama series feature a close community such as a family or a neighbourhood?
- Why are the characters rarely seen outside the community? (Consider the practical constraints.)

Fictions

In the world of fiction, events are tailored to come to a conclusion at the end of each programme. In detective series, the criminals get their come uppance, and disturbing events are finally settled. This is in itself a fiction, for real life is full of loose ends and unfairness.

We are inclined to trust our favourite characters, especially if we identify them as forces for good. Through them, programmes create a fictional world of right and wrong, suggesting what is admirable and what is contemptible. We can't 'see' this fictional world in the way we can 'see' characters and sets, but we are obliged to share it if the programme is to make sense. Dramas usually invite us to take sides with detectives rather than villains, British spies rather than foreign spies, and so on. In siding with them, we are obliged to accept them as whole characters, warts and all. In this way, we excuse their faults, which often include violence and prejudice.

Bear this in mind as you read the following scenes from the *Taggart* episode 'Dead Giveaway', in which a young boxer has been seen staggering drunkenly by the canal before falling into the water. His dead body is now being fished out of the canal while the police question an eyewitness.

Characters:
Taggart – Detective Chief Inspector
Jardine – Detective Sergeant
Laura Campbell – Detective Sergeant
McVitie – Detective Chief Superintendent
Dr Andrews – police doctor
Joe Higginson – the dead boxer
Robert Higginson – his father, a taxi driver
Bill Grieve – runs the Boxing Club

SCENE 8
EXT. CANALBANK
DAY 1   3.30 pm

THE AREA AROUND THE BODY IS TAPED OFF. POLICE ARE FISHING THE BODY OUT, ON TO THE BANK. TAGGART WATCHES AS JOE IS LAID FACE UP ON THE GRASS. TAGGART SEES A WALLET HANGING OUT OF HIS POCKET. HE REMOVES IT, STARTS LOOKING FOR IDENTIFICATION. BEHIND HIM JARDINE TAKES NOTES FROM THE TRAMP.

TRAMP
He was staggering about. All over the place. Drink. Or drugs. Terrible .... at his age.

JARDINE
Can I have your name, please?

TRAMP
Shaugnessy. John. Patrick. Matthew. Constable, sir. I used to be in the Police Force myself. Long time ago. If I can give you some advice, sir, you're going to have trouble with that one. With a drowning, you see, you can't draw a white line around the body.

JARDINE
Address?

TRAMP
No fixed abode, sir.

JARDINE
Isn't it a bit cold for you? This time of year.

TRAMP
It's good of you to care, sir.

Since I reported the body, do you think there could be a reward?

For a cup of tea?

JARDINE GIVES HIM A POUND NOTE.

JARDINE
Make sure it is tea.

TRAMP
I never drink anything else, sir.

JARDINE GOES OVER TO TAGGART WHO HAS FOUND SOME ID IN THE WALLET. AT THE SAME TIME, WE SEE DR ANDREWS APPROACHING.

TAGGART
How much did you give him?

JARDINE
A pound.

TAGGART
What are we, the Sally Army?

JARDINE LOOKS DOWN AT THE BOY'S FACE, RECOGNISES IT.

JARDINE
I know him. It's Joe Higgison. He's in the Church youth clubs – I run on Sunday nights.

DR ANDREWS IS APPROACHED BY THE TRAMP.

TRAMP
Excuse me, sir – as I reported the body, I wondered if there might be a reward –

A UNIFORMED POLICEMAN LEADS HIM AWAY FROM DR ANDREWS.

JUST LIKE LIFE?

SCENE 10
EXT. CANALBANK
DAY 1   3.45 pm

DR ANDREWS FINISHES HIS EXAMINATION OF THE BODY. TURNS TO TAGGART. JARDINE STANDS ALONGSIDE.

DR ANDREWS
Can't smell any alcohol. Your witness said he was swaying —?

TAGGART
That's right.

DR ANDREWS
There is a head injury on the left temple. But of course he could have got that falling in. Or knocked it on a branch. Otherwise, he shows all the signs of drowning.

JARDINE
He wasn't the type.

THEY LOOK AT HIM CURIOUSLY.

JARDINE (continues)
To drink. Or take drugs.

TAGGARD
Lots of kids don't look the type —

JARDINE (ADAMANT)
He wasn't the type. (PAUSE) I've met his parents. I'd like to break the news to them.

TAGGART
Go on then. (PAUSE) While you're at it — ask about drugs. You know the things to look for.

JARDINE LEAVES. FROM THE OTHER DIRECTION LAURA CAMPBELL APPROACHES WITH THE SPORTS BAG. ON THE SIDE IS PRINTED 'BALLATER YOUTH BOXING CLUB'.

LAURA
Sir — we found this downriver. Pair of boxing gloves inside. Could be they're his.

TAGGART
Sensible deduction.

TAGGART OPENS THE BAG AND LOOKS INSIDE AT THE BOXING GLOVES.

SCENE 14
INT. YOUTH BOXING CLUB
DAY 1   4.45 pm

TWO BOYS ARE BOXING. OTHERS ARE TRAINING WITH PUNCH BAGS AND OTHER EQUIPMENT. JARDINE WATCHES THE TWO TEENAGERS WITH SOME DISTASTE. TAGGART TALKS TO BILL GRIEVE.

GRIEVE
Joe? Dead? (PAUSE) He only stayed here twenty minutes. He'd had a row with his girl friend. I think he just came to — box it out of his system.

TAGGART
What was the row about?

GRIEVE
Some youth-hostelling ski trip they were supposed to go on this weekend. To Aviemore. She stood him up at the last minute.

TAGGART
He had a lot of interests.

GRIEVE
It was his parents. Always warring. I think Joe just did anything to get out of the house.

TAGGART
Was drugs one of them?

GRIEVE
Drugs? Joe. Never. I like to think I keep my boys out of trouble like that. I used to be in the Prison service. Tillicoultry Detention Centre.

JARDINE IS STILL WATCHING THE BOXING.

JARDINE
How many knocks did Joe take?

GRIEVE
Punches? I never counted.

JARDINE
To the head?

GRIEVE
A few.

JARDINE
It's possible — he may have suffered from a delayed concussion.

GRIEVE
I wouldn't have let him leave if I'd thought —

TAGGART
It's only one. Of a few possibilities.

JARDINE JUST KEEPS STARING AT THE BOXING BOUT BETWEEN THE TWO BOYS, WHO ARE PUNCHING EACH OTHER ENERGETICALLY.

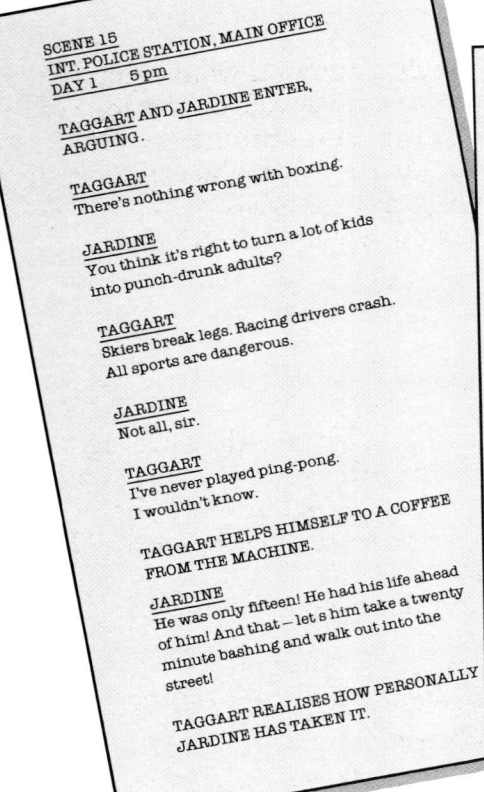

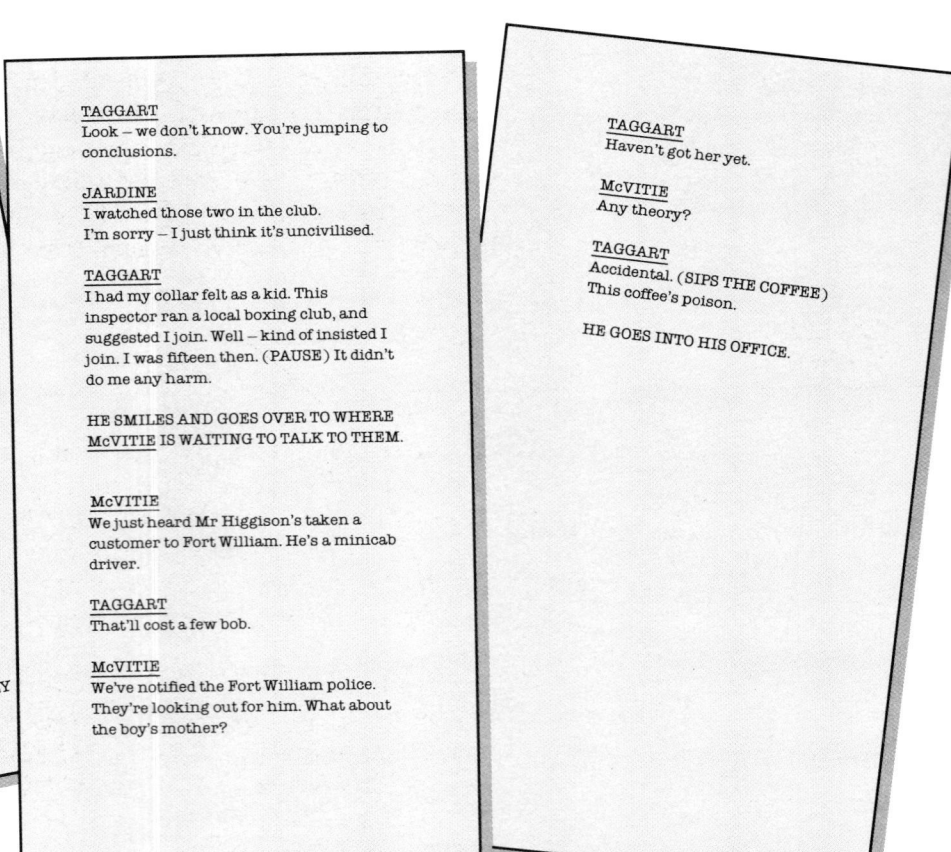

```
SCENE 15
INT. POLICE STATION, MAIN OFFICE
DAY 1    5 pm

TAGGART AND JARDINE ENTER,
ARGUING.

TAGGART
There's nothing wrong with boxing.

JARDINE
You think it's right to turn a lot of kids
into punch-drunk adults?

TAGGART
Skiers break legs. Racing drivers crash.
All sports are dangerous.

JARDINE
Not all, sir.

TAGGART
I've never played ping-pong.
I wouldn't know.

TAGGART HELPS HIMSELF TO A COFFEE
FROM THE MACHINE.

JARDINE
He was only fifteen! He had his life ahead
of him! And that – let s him take a twenty
minute bashing and walk out into the
street!

TAGGART REALISES HOW PERSONALLY
JARDINE HAS TAKEN IT.
```

```
TAGGART
Look – we don't know. You're jumping to
conclusions.

JARDINE
I watched those two in the club.
I'm sorry – I just think it's uncivilised.

TAGGART
I had my collar felt as a kid. This
inspector ran a local boxing club, and
suggested I join. Well – kind of insisted I
join. I was fifteen then. (PAUSE) It didn't
do me any harm.

HE SMILES AND GOES OVER TO WHERE
McVITIE IS WAITING TO TALK TO THEM.

McVITIE
We just heard Mr Higgison's taken a
customer to Fort William. He's a minicab
driver.

TAGGART
That'll cost a few bob.

McVITIE
We've notified the Fort William police.
They're looking out for him. What about
the boy's mother?
```

```
TAGGART
Haven't got her yet.

McVITIE
Any theory?

TAGGART
Accidental. (SIPS THE COFFEE)
This coffee's poison.

HE GOES INTO HIS OFFICE.
```

- What can you deduce about Taggart's attitude towards:
    - Jardine
    - institutions such as the church, family, and the police force
    - human nature
- Compare the characters of Taggart and Jardine.
- Which of Taggart's personal qualities make him a successful police officer?
- How admirable do you find these qualities in other people?
- What methods and information does Taggart use to pursue his investigation?
- What problems might arise if real police officers operated in this way?

Television detectives are protected by the scriptwriter: in solving cases, their intuition is always successful and their mistakes are minor. Does this give viewers a false impression of crime detection and police attitudes? More importantly, does it give the viewer a false impression of human nature and how to deal with it?

Answers to science fiction film sets

| 1 | *Forbidden Planet*, 1956 | 3 | *Alien*, 1979 |
| 2 | *The Forbin Project*, 1970 | 4 | *The Shape of Things To Come*, 1936 |

Storytelling

Storytelling is an art. A skilled storyteller knows how to whet the appetite, hold attention and have readers or viewers on the edge of their seats. We are quick to recognise the skills of someone who reads aloud well, who can tell a good anecdote, or who can build up a 'shaggy dog' story. But do we always notice the art of the programme makers as they draw us in to a television drama?

Titles

The television programme maker has us hooked in the opening seconds. Even before the first scene, the title excites the imagination. The programme title *You Must Be The Husband* gives a light-hearted impression of a couple whose relationship is off-beat. The 'off-the-cuff' wording hints at comedy.

Study the wording of these programme titles:

Hot Metal
Are You Being Served?
The Charmer
Just Good Friends
Wish Me Luck
Hooperman
Star Trek
LA Law
CATS Eyes
Yes, Prime Minister
The Sullivans
Hill Street Blues
The Hitchhiker's Guide to the Galaxy
Thin Air

- What does each title lead you to expect from the programme which follows?
- Compare your answers with the programme outlines on page 25.
- If you know any of these programmes, can you account for the choice of titles? In what way do they pinpoint the essence of the programmes?

Television drama covers a wide variety of programming. In a group, compile a list of all the drama programmes you know under the following headings:

Situation comedies	e.g.	*Just Good Friends*
Detectives/cops	e.g.	*Hill Street Blues*
Soap operas	e.g.	*The Sullivans*
Drama serials	e.g.	*The Charmer*
Science fiction	e.g.	*Star Trek*

- Do you notice any common themes or features in the titles of different types of programme? Soap opera titles, for example, invariably feature a family or location. The reason is simple: soap operas are always based on families or enclosed communities.

Title sequences

The title itself is packaged within the title sequence of the programme. Like a book cover, the title sequence excites our interest by dropping hints of the pleasures to come. Each has its own style. Soap operas use sequences which are usually brief and obvious, with distinctive catchy music to beckon the regular viewer.

- Watch a handful of title sequences closely and use slow-motion to study the details.
- Discuss the image of the programme which is conveyed in the title sequence, explaining in particular:

    — the choice of music — the pace
    — the selection of images — the appearance of the title itself

- Prepare a storyboard title sequence, 8–10 frames long, suitable for the following programmes. (You can find an explanation and advice about storyboards on page 129.)

Beachcombers – a drama serial. The tide washes ashore the telltale clues of a recent wreckage at sea. Soon the family who work this remote beach find themselves involved in intrigue and suspense.

Sleeping Partners – a situation comedy. A business merger brings a new partner to Beetlehall Manufacturing Co. Ltd – and soon the sparks are flying between the new whizz-kid director, Jill, and the long-established Jack. Their dramatic clashes hide one little secret . . . at home, they are husband and wife.

Time Police – science fiction. The crack squad of AD 3003 travel in time to avert disasters and crimes which threaten the planet's destiny. Their undercover work through the centuries must be discreet, for tampering with history has its dangers . . .

The grammar of television pictures

When we read a book, we expect and accept the conventions of grammar: the story is told in sentences, paragraphs, chapters. So, too, in television. Although the rules of television grammar may be unspoken, we are just as familiar with them. The basic punctuation mark is the *cut*. This is simply where the picture changes because the camera has been repositioned, perhaps to signify a shift in time or place.

- Look carefully over the cuts shown opposite and say what each one represents, for example,

    — a change of camera angle — a shift in place
    — a shift in time — or any combination of these

JUST LIKE LIFE?

- The cut is very common. Watch two minutes of a drama programme and count the number of cuts. Does the number surprise you?
- Watch a couple of minutes from other types of programme, for example,

    – an interview
    – a pop music show
    – a story-reading for very young children

- What differences do you notice in the frequency of cuts in these programmes?
- How do you account for them?

But the cut is not the only form of 'punctuation' used on television. There are also *mixes, wipes, fades to black*, and a range of video effects, where the picture slides, tumbles, or shatters off the screen. They all have different meanings.

The two sketches below each represent several seconds from a television sequence. Study these alternative links between shots, then answer the questions which follow.

ON THE SOFA, THE COUPLE DRAW CLOSE, GAZING INTO EACH OTHER'S EYES...THEY ARE ABOUT TO KISS...	CUT	A MESSENGER CARRYING A PARCEL IS RINGING THE DOORBELL.
AS ABOVE	MIX — THE PICTURE DISSOLVES FROM ONE SHOT TO THE NEXT.	AS ABOVE
	FADE DOWN AND UP — THE FIRST PICTURE FADES DOWN TO BLACK. THE SECOND PICTURE FADES UP	

- What difference does each link make to the meaning of the scene?
- What, if anything, do you imagine happening between the shots?
- What do you imagine the next shot would be in each case?
- Attempt to define the meaning of the *mix* and the *fade to black*.

Tricks with time

Television plays tricks with time. This isn't simply because the story has to be squeezed into a 25-minute slot, but because all fiction selects and streamlines material to the storyline. It would be very confusing to include scenes which were entirely irrelevant and even boring. If the camera shows our hero asleep, we expect his slumber to be suddenly shattered by an urgent telephone call. We would be quite put out to watch ten minutes of snoring.

As we watch, the brain works immediately to interpret the transition from one shot to the next. One is hardly aware of reading the clues to estimate the time gap. The process is more amazing when one realises that one cut alone could signify a change in time, place, and camera position – so the brain sifts the various possibilities very quickly.

Television is skilled in condensing time. Try it for yourself:

First, imagine you are making a 25-minute drama programme about the joy and tension of a wedding day. It is to be lightly comic, as it follows the events of the wedding day from dawn to dusk. Clearly, you can't show everything in that time. Make a list of the events you want to include in the programme.

Secondly, choose a drama programme you have seen very recently, such as an episode of a soap opera or a serial. Imagine you have to show a one-minute résumé of the programme as an introduction to the next episode, to bring absent viewers up to date. Which snippets would you use?

- In each case, how did you decide which material to include?
- Think of occasions when time is condensed on television, for example,

    — losing time between episodes of a soap opera
    — editing the selected highlights of a football match
    — making a promotion (trailer) for forthcoming programmes

- What special problems are posed by 'losing time' in each case and how do production teams deal with them?

Answers to programme outlines

Hot Metal Situation comedy about a tabloid newspaper.
Are You Being Served? Situation comedy set in a department store.
The Charmer Drama serial about a murderous womaniser and confidence trickster of the 1940s.
Just Good Friends Situation comedy about a couple whose relationship never quite rekindles.
Wish Me Luck Drama serial about women undercover agents in wartime France.
Hooperman American detective series.
Star Trek Popular science fiction series about the adventures of the Starship Enterprise.
LA Law American drama series based on a Los Angeles legal practice.
CATS Eyes Cop series based on a team of women private detectives.
Yes, Prime Minister Situation comedy based on political machinations behind the scenes at Downing Street.
The Sullivans Australian soap opera based on a large family.
Hill Street Blues Cop series based on events at a police station in a tough district of New York.
The Hitchhiker's Guide to the Galaxy Comic science fiction serial following the exploits of Arthur Dent when he is whisked into space by a friendly alien.
Thin Air Drama serial about murder and intrigue at a radio station.

Stories

Television is full of stories, ranging from soap opera to Shakespeare. Stories invite us into an imaginary world which may look familiar, but which is a fiction. We allow ourselves to enter it, safe in the knowledge that its twists and turns will be resolved by the end of the programme.

The world of drama is an idealised world. In comedy, the worst of mishaps never does serious damage. It is all 'in fun'. In detective series, good always triumphs over evil, and everyone gets their just deserts. No real person leads a life so full of fascinating personal intrigue as does a character in a soap opera. In fiction, time never hangs heavy. It is a world of condensed action, intense, purposeful and involving. The events are selected, shaped, and organised in a way real life is not.

- Consider these events and people. How are they commonly presented in television fiction? Think of examples you have seen recently.

  - shootings
  - solving crimes
  - Northerners
  - teachers and students
  - hospital
  - relationships in a neighbourhood
  - flat sharing
  - business women
  - husbands of successful women
  - mothers-in-law
  - Cockneys
  - used car salesmen

Doorstep salesmen: a fair stereotype?

- Contrast the television portrayal with real-life equivalents.
- What dangers are raised by stereotypes?

Television drama presents life which has been directed and shaped for our entertainment. It may well shock us in its presentation of crime, violence and conflict, but it also protects us from unseemly realism. An obvious example is the presentation of shootings on television. Death is shown in sanitised form – a quick clean bullet – and murder rarely goes unpunished. Some people argue that such protection 'desensitises' viewers by inviting them to take violence lightly, but many aspects of television drama are symbolic rather than realistic. 'Shoot-out' scenes do not aim to provide a detailed study of death, only to portray its occurrence.

More worrying are the long-term effects of such pictures. If television dwells on sex and violence, does it create a climate in which rape, murder and abuse become more acceptable?

Plot development

All stories have shape. One of the pleasures of watching television drama is anticipating the course of events and the movement of the plot towards its climax, passing through moments of suspense and tension, surprise, relief and conclusion. Different types of story have their own rhythms which we come to know well.

Consider these stories and suggest how they might continue:

(a) Our police heroes are parked sneakily in a side road, watching for speeding vehicles on the main road, when their radio alerts them to an armed bank robbery. At that moment, the squeal of tyres and a glimpse of the getaway car tells them that the robbers are making off with the loot. Without hesitation, the police set off in pursuit.

- Describe the pursuit. Mention some details. How does it end?

(b) Towards the end of a popular soap opera, the sad figure of Lily is seen returning home earlier than expected to confront her wayward husband, Rick. Things haven't been going too well recently. There's just 30 seconds to the end of this week's episode.

- What happens in these closing moments?

(c) The loony with the bomb is sweating profusely, rambling incoherently, and is very twitchy. Everyone in the place is terrified. Attempts to reason with him only incense him further. Soon he will break. They could all die. The greatest caution is necessary. Enter our hero.

- How does our hero deal with the situation? Mention some details. How does it all end?

Now consider the following questions:

- How do you work out the likely development of the plots?
- What factors influence the development of the plot at any particular moment?

Consider this scene and how it might develop:

The bank robbery is going according to plan until Arthur Plugg, the timid bank clerk, refuses to divulge the safe combination.

- How would you expect the scene to unfold in the following cases:
    1. In a soap opera (Arthur Plugg may be a familiar character).
    2. In a situation comedy.
    3. In a detective thriller.

All stories belong to a tradition, and viewers have surprisingly strict expectations about how they should develop. Writers face the problem of creating new dramas which retain successful elements of the tradition, while introducing new twists to refresh the audience. Comedy, in particular, relies on a knowledge of tradition. We are often invited to laugh at characters whose scenes do not turn out as expected.

Storylining

Television drama imposes further demands on writers because it must be worked into fixed periods of time. On a commercial station, allowances must also be made for the advertising breaks. Even more demanding is writing for programmes which continue from episode to episode – as in soap opera or serial drama.

- **What difficulties do writers face in creating stories structured in episodes?**
- **How do writers encourage the viewer to tune in to the next episode?**

In long-running serials, the writing team will prepare a storyline for several weeks or months ahead before individual writers produce a detailed script. Important events and changes of characters can be built up several episodes in advance.

- Think of examples where:
    - characters have been written out
    - characters have been introduced
    - characters have been 'rested'
- How was each managed?

Try it yourself. Here is the storyline for one episode of a soap opera about the turbulent relationship between two families:

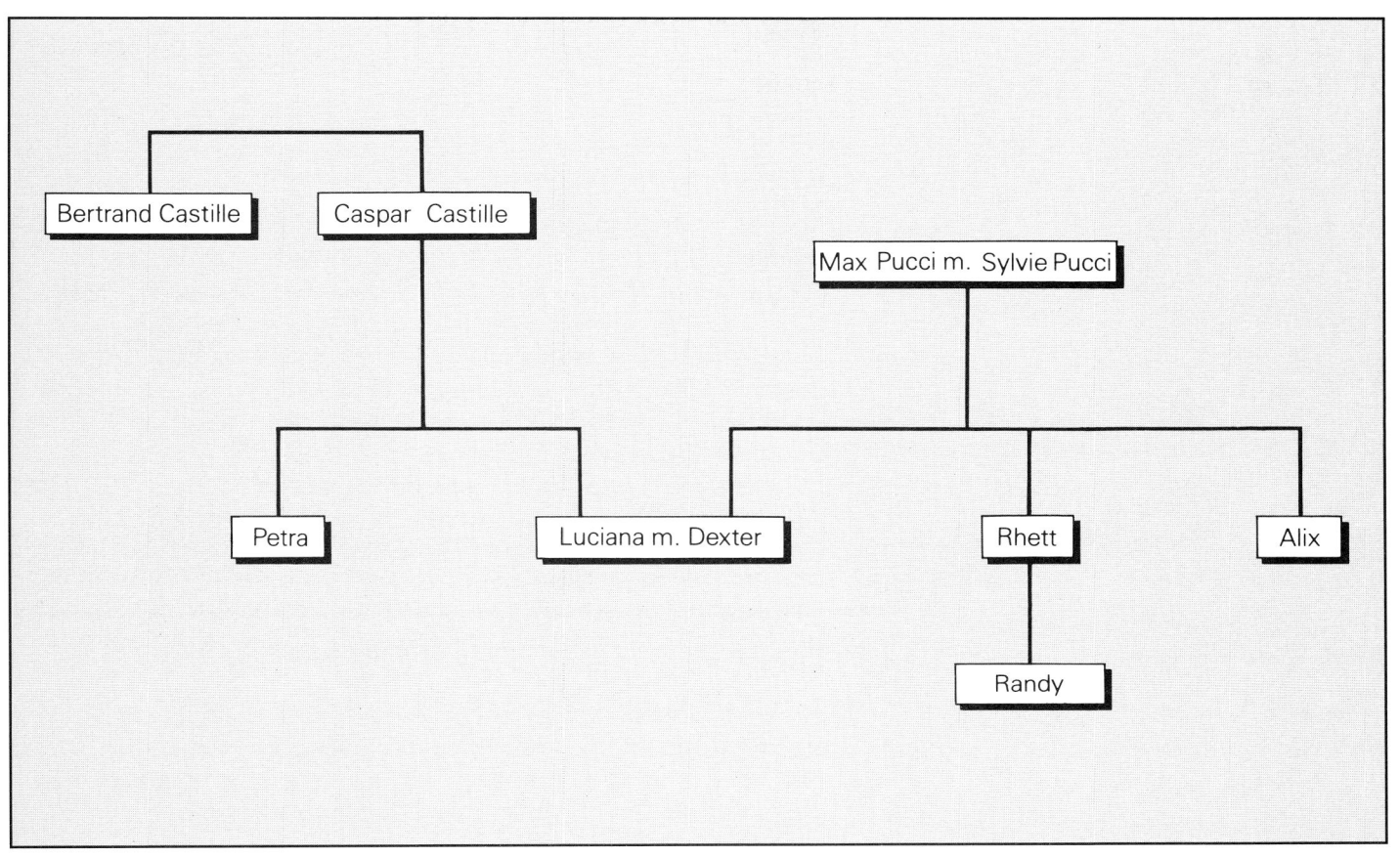

```
Bertrand Castille ── Caspar Castille                    Max Pucci m. Sylvie Pucci
                          │                                        │
          ┌───────────────┴────────┐              ┌────────────────┼──────────┐
        Petra              Luciana m. Dexter    Rhett                        Alix
                                                  │
                                                Randy
```

Caspar Castille has forbidden Petra to see Rhett. Although the affair was not serious, Petra is now determined to have her own way. She begs her sister Luciana to help her smuggle a note to Rhett through her husband, Dexter. Dexter is infuriated by her involvement and an argument ensues. In any case, Rhett has vanished, following a new lead in the search for his son Randy, the child of his first marriage, who was kidnapped three episodes back.

Meanwhile, Max Pucci has finally succeeded in buying up 51 per cent of the shares in Castille International Trading. He visits the Castille office to gloat over his defeated rival.

Dexter flies to the conference in Geneva. He is clearly attracted by the alluring but strangely familiar Loretta da Palma. But who is the mysterious stranger she meets by night after leaving Dexter? And where is Rhett, missing for two days now? And why is Petra packing her cases?

- Using this storyline as your starting point, either improvise a scene by acting it out or write a script for it.
- Write a storyline for the next episode.
- Discuss the familiar twists and turns in soap opera stories, especially those which centre on:

  – pregnancy and children
  – the ups and downs of marriage
  – terrible accidents
  – business and financial problems
  – the past coming to light

- Bearing in mind the practical aspects of sustaining a serial story over the years, can you account for the frequent appearance of these stock events in soap operas?

Endings

- Discuss which words would best fit the gaps below:

> We know what endings to expect because we are familiar with how the plots in different (1) _____ develop. If we are watching a (2) _____, we expect the writer to leave us in suspense, so that we tune in for the next (3) _____. If we are watching a (4) _____ or a one-off drama, it would be reasonable to expect a conclusive ending. Traditionally, the problems which started the plot rolling are finally (5) _____, the loose ends are tied up, the mysterious details are made clear, the good characters are rewarded with success, (6) _____ and/or (7) _____. The characters who have behaved badly can expect to be (8) _____, (9) _____, or even (10) _____. Unless, of course, there is to be a (11) _____, in which case an opening will be left to restart the plot at a later date.

There are several correct answers. Compare yours with the list on page 144.

Endings make fiction whole and self-contained. Each story has a beginning, a middle and an end. Justice is always passed on the characters. Events come to rest. It is all very definite and reassuring, unlike life, which is always unfolding. Fiction is a form of reassurance through which we shape the world.

The Craft of Fiction

Creating a programme is a craft. An idea takes shape first as a script, materialises in the design and performance, and is finally moulded into a programme in the editing suite. The cameras, scripts and editing equipment are tools of the job. In much the same way as a sculptor uses marble or a painter uses paint, the programme team works with pictures and sounds. There are many levels of creativity: generating ideas and scripts; directing actors and designing sets; placing cameras and selecting shots; organising and pruning the material in editing.

Scripts

Television drama usually starts out as a script which looks very like a play script – the sort you will have come across before. It is, however, a mistake to think of television drama as adapted for television from the theatre. A new generation of writers has grown up writing specifically for television. They write with television in mind, seeing the scenes unfold on a 'mental screen'. In this way, they play to the strengths of television and avoid its pitfalls.

> I get ideas for *Taggart* in lots of different places – sometimes from sitting in the public gallery of the High Court watching a case go on, from a story that's been in the newspapers, sometimes even from wandering round a location that attracts me (that will often give me an idea for the start of a story).
>
> A writer has to think visually and not just think in terms of words, of dialogue. I plot *Taggart* out to look as visual as possible, and in many cases after I've written the scene, I will totally strip away the dialogue because I think the image says everything.
>
> The main rule of the game in popular drama is to entertain. People sometimes sniff at popular drama because it is popular – but if I were to take a real police investigation and write about it as it really happened, I would show detectives sitting at their desks dealing with 500–600 statements from eyewitnesses. I think the Great British Audience would fall asleep, no matter how real it was. Popular drama has got to take reality and turn it into another kind of reality.
>
> **Glenn Chandler, Scriptwriter of *Taggart* (Scottish Television)**

Once a script is complete, the work of the writer is finished and the director takes over. It is the responsibility of the director to develop a *camera script* for use on the set. At this point, the programme takes on a practical dimension. Ideas must be expressed in terms of lighting, camerawork, acting and design. The test of a good script is how well it lends itself to the medium.

Visualising the scene

An active visual imagination is essential in a director. He or she must first enact the scene in the mind's eye to see how it will look on television, then work out where to put the cameras. There are practical constraints: the number of cameras involved (much drama is shot using just one camera); the type of location; the lighting and so on.

In televising a scene, the director has to find ways of coping with seemingly impossible demands. Twenty minutes has to be shrunk into a few seconds. Certain actions have to be implied rather than shown. Here are some common problems for the camera. Visualise how you would shoot these scenes, considering both vision and sound:

Walking down a corridor, entering a room and then sitting at a desk.
- Clumsy in one long take. How many shots would it take to do this? When would you break the action to move the camera and where would you place it for each shot?

Someone waiting in a queue for ages.
- How do you communicate the dreariness without putting your audience through it?

Someone looking at a particular person in a crowd.
- How do you identify the observer and the observed?

A person enters through a door and an interviewer asks a question.
- How do you get the interviewer into the picture?

A character flies to Paris and has a brief business meeting.
- How do you do this without massive expense and hassle?

A character in a car crash.
- How do you do it without the risk and bother of actually crashing a car?

A villain enters a crowded room with a hidden gun.
- How do you make clear it's a villain and imply the presence of the hidden gun?

A conversation in which one party is feeling nervous and guilty.
- What details will the camera 'notice' to ensure the audience recognises the guilt?

A thief is holding up a bank. Meanwhile, a police car speeds towards the scene of the crime.
- How do you make clear that the two scenes are taking place simultaneously?

> **The unsuspecting victim is alone in the huge house. Outside, an evil presence stalks the garden.**
> - How do you build up the tension? How do you suggest the presence of evil?

Television uses these tricks all the time. We become familiar with them and accept them. They are television conventions. They help both the director and the viewer to create the meaning of a scene.

Locations

In a studio, sets are purpose built to leave room for the cameras to move around, but outside locations pose a different problem. Places have to be found which will accommodate cameras in adequate sound and lighting conditions.

- Suggest suitable locations to shoot the following scenes within a mile of your present position:
    - A car chase, ending in a dead-end street, followed by a chase through private gardens.
    - A thief concealing his loot underwater, away from prying eyes.
    - A wedding.
    - A family on a country picnic.
    - A busy shopping expedition.
    - A multi-millionaire arriving at impressive business headquarters.
    - A dark place for a meeting between two spies.
- Name appropriate locations.
- What problems do you anticipate in using these locations? Make a list.
- How could you improvise if an appropriate location could not be found?
- Think of four different locations for the same scene between a detective and an informer, to meet these requirements:
    1. The scene must have a seedy and sinister atmosphere.
    2. The informer does not want the detective to recognise him. He wants to pass on his information without fear of being followed or overheard by anyone else.
    3. A scene full of tension, close to the climax of the programme, with an atmosphere of urgency, danger and violence.
    4. The two wish to meet without drawing attention to themselves and where they can't be 'bugged'.
- What technical problems does each location pose for the director?

Camerawork

In the past, much television drama was shot on film, using a single camera. Nowadays, drama is often shot in the same way, but recorded onto videotape rather than film. Videotape has the advantage of being cheap, reusable and easy to copy, though the tone of the picture is not always as subtle. This technique is called single-camera working. A scene is shot several times, each time from a different angle, and the final version is edited together to contain a variety of shots. It is a method with several advantages: the best performances can be selected, the set is not cluttered with cameras, and the choice of angles is greater.

For many years, single-camera working was technically impossible on videotape. The video cameras were too bulky to carry around and the editing was complex and slow. Instead, television studios used the multi-camera technique, using four or five cameras and cutting from one shot to another as the scene was recorded. The job of cutting 'live' from one camera to another was done by a *vision mixer*.

Multi-camera working is still used because not all types of programme are suited to single-camera working. Consider the following:

— a horse race
— a live music show
— an interview
— a drama serial
— a quiz

- Which of these requires (a) single-camera working, (b) multi-camera working?
- Which might be shot using either technique?

Now consider the following scenes, and how you would shoot them:

(a) A kitchen. A disastrous dinner party in the next room. Nothing is going right. The hostess is fumbling about looking for the serving plate. Heaps of dirty dishes collapse. The cat is licking the cream off the trifle and is shooed away — too late. Someone calls through, 'Everything all right in there, darling?' Suddenly, the hostess spots smoke billowing from the oven. Opens it. As the clouds subside, it becomes clear that the roast is a cinder.

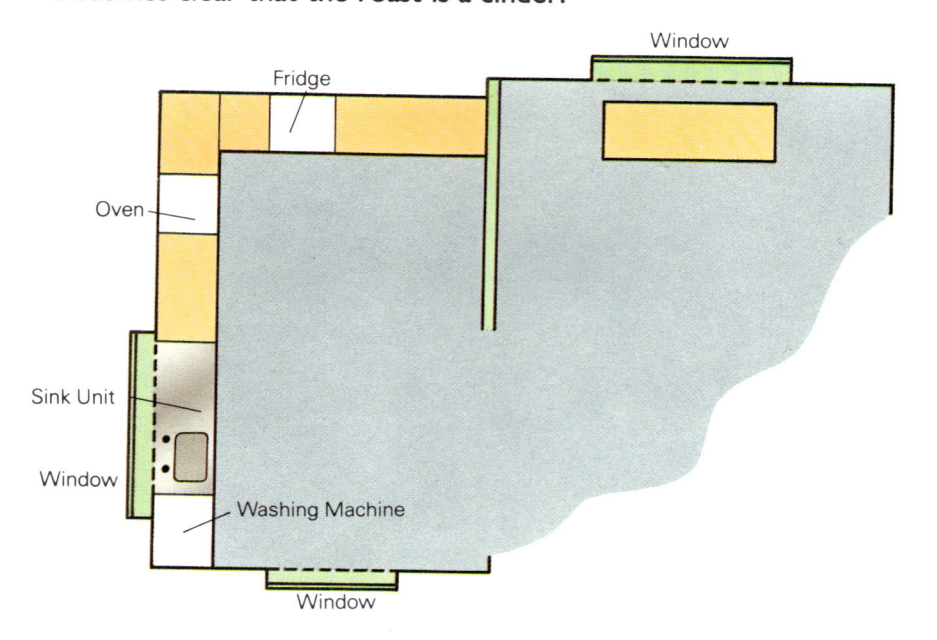

Set for kitchen scene

- You have two fixed cameras for this scene, which cannot be moved. You can zoom in and out as you like and cut between them as necessary.
- Imagine this scene in seven or eight shots.
- What will the shots be? Write a one-line description or draw a cartoon storyboard.
- Mark onto the plan the position of the two cameras.
- What limitations are imposed by the set and the number of cameras?

(b) In a train. The parent and child are sitting by the window. The child is thirsty and asks for a can of lemonade. The parent allows the child to go up the train to the buffet. Twenty minutes later, the child has not returned and the parent is worried. The parent asks a neighbour to watch over their things and heads up the train to the buffet. The staff at the counter say they have not seen the child.

Set for train scene

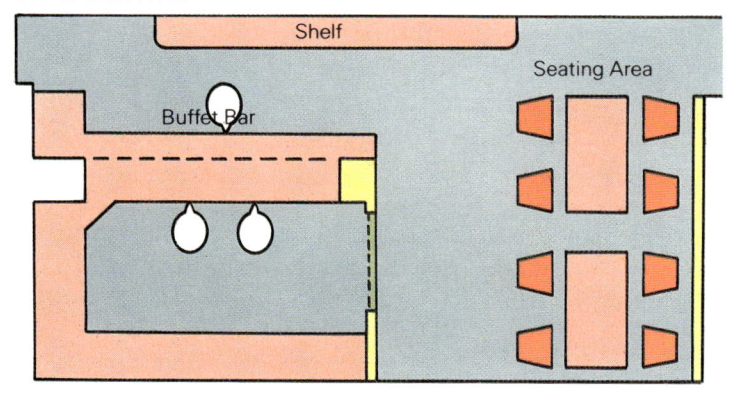

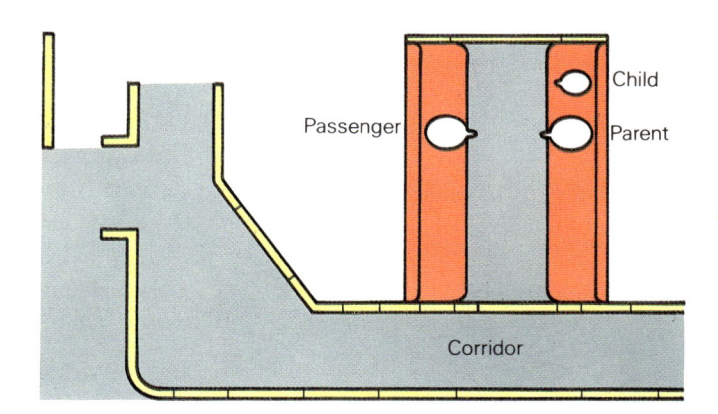

- You have a single hand-held camera which can be moved about as much as you like.
- Imagine this scene in no more than ten shots.
- What will the shots be? Write a one-line description or draw a cartoon storyboard.
- How do you indicate the passing of 20 minutes? (It need not be exact.)
- How do you deal with the parent's journey up the train without sending your audience to sleep?
- What limitations are imposed by the set?

When you have written the camera scripts for these two scenes, you can compare your ideas with those of a professional television director, shown on page 37.

Much more complicated is this scene which appears in the *Taggart* episode 'Dead Giveaway'.

Two men have mounted a fork-lift truck and are making their way down a huge aisle of storage shelves in a book warehouse. Cochrane is driving, while Knowles rides on the elevated platform. Suddenly, Cochrane suffers a violent choking fit; he has been poisoned. He collapses onto the controls and the vehicle careers forwards out of control, along the narrow aisle of books. The original script for what happens next is on the next page.

KNOWLES REALISES THE DANGER HE IS IN ON THE ASCENDING PLATFORM AND LEAPS OFF ON TO THE HIGH SHELVES.

THE FORK-LIFT TRUCK CAREERS TO THE END OF THE AISLE.

WAREHOUSE WORKERS HAVE TO LEAP OUT OF THE WAY.

THE RUNAWAY FORK-LIFT TRUCK CRASHES INTO A HUGE PILE OF CARDBOARD BOXES, FULL OF BOOKS.

Simple? Well, try it. How do you imagine this scene played out on television in an exciting and visual manner? A clue: the director used twelve shots.

When you have tried this mental exercise, turn to page 40 and consider the camera script used by the director.

The director

The director is the most important person present during the recording of the scene, controlling the entire production team and thus our interpretation of the drama. Our view of the scene is determined by what the director chooses to show us, and the way in which it is shown.

Read this transcript of the director's comments made during the recording and editing of the warehouse scene above, and then answer the questions that follow:

During shooting:

> And Action!... Cut!... Can you get yourself into position like that? Yeah, like that. See this, going away from you as it were, you get a better impression of danger that way... and Action!... Now, just a close up of Gareth just about to jump... Can we do that now, do you think?... The jump, yes... That's the one, that's the position, there... okay, do you see that, Lewis? Do you want to line up on that?... Right, turn over! Turn over! Action!... Em, I wonder if it's worth doing another one but from another angle? Or do you think you've got it?... But from your point of view, is it Gareth or is it... I think I'd better take one other angle...

During editing:

> Er, what happens there? It's too slow that, isn't it?... Well, we could speed that up, just that shot. We'll send it to the laboratory and make them speed it up, because the effect's not there... So everything's nice there, everything's fast, then suddenly it all slows down... That just needs to be very fast... The sound, it's coming to a halt isn't it? We could re-dub the sound on that, and make it sound as though it's really steaming ahead. We could even make it sound faster.

- Deduce from the transcript:

    (a) What are the chief responsibilities of the director?
    (b) Who else is at work and what are their jobs?

Editing

Editing is the process of sorting and arranging the recorded material into a finished programme. The director and editor end up with a programme tailored to the particular time slot, and constructed to have pace, shape and dramatic rhythm.

> We shoot the scene from many different angles. It's easier for the editor to build up the excitement if he's got a wide variation of shots. The idea is that even a small sequence should have a beginning, a middle and an end. We start slowly and build in pace throughout, and choose a strong shot to finish on. The sound is actually as important as the pictures. If you listen to a sequence with no sound whatsoever, it would be very dull. Music heightens the drama: it is the icing on the cake.
>
> **Alan MacMillan, Director of *Taggart* (Scottish Television)**

A drama shot on one camera has to be pieced together picture by picture. It is painstaking work. A studio recording which went well on the day, using several cameras, can be much quicker to edit. But in each case the editor's job is to construct a programme which has visual style and dramatic tempo.

A professional view

Here, television director Terry Kinane shows how he would approach the scenes described on pages 34–5. The camera positions are shown on the set plans on page 39.

Kitchen scene

Shot 1 Camera 1
Wide shot to establish the kitchen. In the foreground left of frame we see the sink unit with some dirty dishes heaped too high. In the background right of the shot we see the hostess. She is looking in cupboards above the fridge.

Shot 2 Cam 2
Mid shot of hostess looking in cupboards.

Shot 3 Cam 1
Wide shot as before. We see some plates topple and fall. The hostess turns on hearing the noise. We contain her move downstage.

Shot 4 Cam 2
A cat has jumped up onto the worktop on top of the fridge. As we pan left with the cat, we discover a large bowl of trifle. The cat starts to eat it.

Shot 5 Cam 1
Two shot – we see the hostess foreground right and the cat eating the trifle in the background left of frame. The hostess notices the cat, and moves towards it. We contain her move upstage. She shoos off

the cat. We hear an off-camera voice: 'Everything all right in there, darling?' A suitable reaction from the hostess. She starts to smell something and looks sharply to her right.

Shot 6 Cam 2
Close up of smoke filled oven.

Shot 7 Cam 1
Loose mid shot of hostess with oven top foreground. Contain her move to the oven, and see her take burnt roast out of it.

Shot 8 Cam 2
Medium close up of hostess as she raises her eyes to heaven.

Train scene

Shot 1 **Position A**
Establishing shot of set. Mother and child right of frame, another passenger left of frame reading a book.

Shot 2 **Pos B**
Two shot of mother and child over shoulder of passenger. As child rises, pan right to entrance of carriage.

Shot 3 **Pos B**
Mid shot of mother getting out a book to read. A bookmark tells us that she has nearly finished the book.

Shot 4 **Pos C**
Mid shot of the passenger opposite the mother, also reading.

Shot 5 **Pos B**
Mid shot. Mother looks at her watch and starts to read book.

Slow mix to shot 6

Shot 6 **Pos B**
Close up of book as mother closes it. Ease out to mid shot mother as she looks at her watch again, worried about her child. Let her rise out of frame.

Shot 7 **Pos A**
Wide shot of carriage. Let her exit frame left.

Shot 8 **Pos D**
Long shot as mother makes her way up corridor. Let her leave frame.

Shot 9 **Pos D (reverse of shot 8)**
Empty frame showing entrance to Buffet Bar. Allow mother into frame and see her enter Buffet Bar. She crosses to counter to talk to staff.

Shot 10 **Pos E**
Close up mother's reaction on hearing that they have not seen her child.

JUST LIKE LIFE?

Set for kitchen scene, showing camera positions

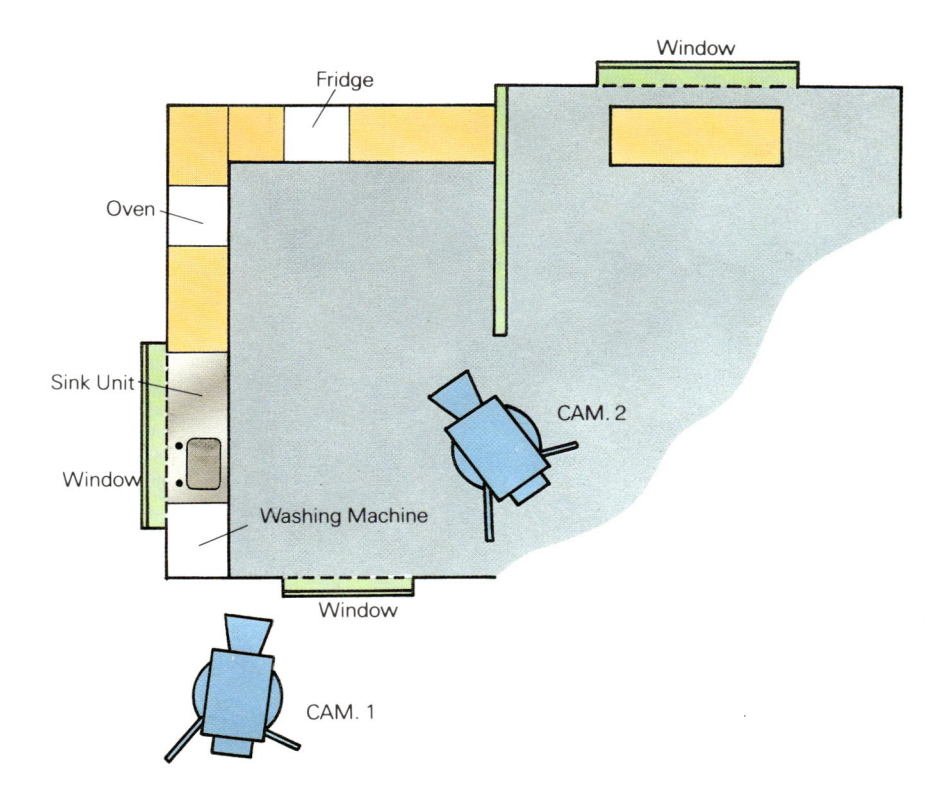

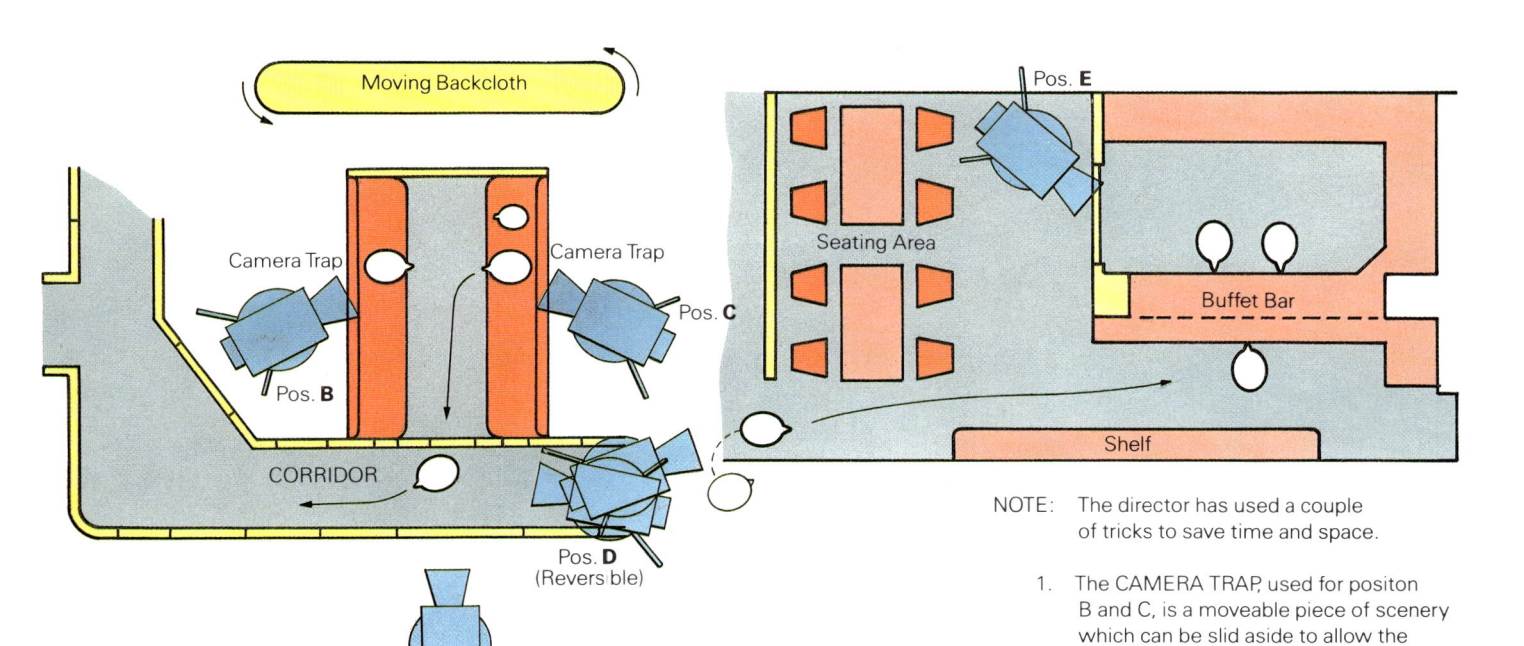

(Diagram labels: Fridge, Window, Oven, Sink Unit, Window, Washing Machine, Window, CAM. 2, CAM. 1)

Set for train scene, showing camera positions

(Diagram labels: Moving Backcloth, Camera Trap, Camera Trap, Pos. B, Pos. C, CORRIDOR, Pos. D (Reversible), Pos. A, Pos. E, Seating Area, Buffet Bar, Shelf)

NOTE: The director has used a couple of tricks to save time and space.

1. The CAMERA TRAP, used for position B and C, is a moveable piece of scenery which can be slid aside to allow the camera to frame the scene.

2. The set for the buffet bar is adjacent to the carriage set. Position D serves for both shots 8 and 9, by reversing the camera.

3. The moving backcloth would be painted to simulate the train speeding through the countryside.

Camera script for warehouse scene

1. Mid shot of Knowles leaping from the fork-lift truck.
2. Low angle long shot looking up at Knowles clinging to the shelves.
3. Close up of Knowles watching the runaway fork-lift truck.
4. Long shot of fork-lift truck receding down the aisle, with Knowles still visible, clinging to the shelves.
5. Reverse angle mid shot of workers fleeing from the approaching truck.
6. Long shot from the roof of the fork-lift truck, showing the fleeing workers.
7. Close up of Cochrane choking.
8. Long shot from the roof of the truck as it approaches a huge stack of boxes. A worker flees to the right.
9. Reverse angle close up of the truck bearing down on the boxes.
10. Mid shot of Cochrane slumped at the controls a second before impact.
11. Close up of the boxes from the roof of the truck at the point of impact.
12. Reverse angle long shot from high above the stack of boxes as the truck bursts through and the stack collapses.

Now answer the following questions:

- In what ways has the director developed the writer's script?
- What kind of detail has he provided for the camera operator?
- Study the camera instructions and the ordering of shots carefully and discuss the director's reason for each choice.

Special Project: Five-Minute Theatre

The object of the exercise

The object of this practical activity is to entertain a small specific audience with a five-minute drama on video.

Aims

1 To gain an inside understanding of televisual drama and in particular, the role of camerawork, narrative techniques, design, performance and scripting.

2 To gain confidence from experience in:
- operating video equipment
- writing, designing and appearing on video
- co-operating in teamwork
- taking responsibilities and making decisions

Advance preparations

1 *Select an audience and a subject.* Break into groups, depending on the video equipment available and decide your choice of video.
Either: A sequence of comic sketches to amuse local primary school pupils.
Or: A short play to show to parents at Parents' Evening. You can write your own short script or ask your teacher about the availability of a ready scripted scene. There are suitable scenes in theatre plays if you are prepared to adapt them. An ambitious but interesting idea is to adapt a scene from a novel. This raises important questions about the strengths and limitations of different media.
Brainstorm for ideas. Get hold of texts if necessary and read through them.

2 Fix a convenient *date* for making the video. Have a fall-back date if it involves outdoor shooting, in case it rains.

3 Find out what video *equipment* is available and book it, along with extra rooms and materials as necessary.

4 Obtain any *permissions* in advance, for example to record particular events or places.

On the day

1 *Collect the video equipment.*

2 *Prepare a 'signing out' list,* so that the teacher will know who is where at any particular moment. Always sign out before you leave the classroom.

3 Work out a *timetable* for the day's activities based on your outline. Leave time to view and discuss the video at the end.

4 *If you are working from a script*, read through the script and discuss the problems of adapting it for video. You may need to cut or modify it.
   Before recording, your script should be marked up to show where the cuts will be, and where the camera will move to.

Imagine the scene as it will appear on the screen. Remember that long static shots are very dull to watch, so you will probably need more cuts than you expect. Vary the distance and position of the camera. Show the reactions of other people and details of the scene, rather than forever watching the face of the person speaking. These are all techniques which make the flow of images more varied.

5 *If you are writing your own script*, think television. Don't write a script and then adapt it for the screen. As you write the dialogue, imagine the shot that will accompany it in the finished version. Bear in mind the range of settings, actors, props and costumes available. If you consider these factors now, it will make recording very much easier.

It is useful if your script is accompanied by camera instructions or a storyboard.

6 Divide your script into sections and *rehearse and record* them individually. Advice about the allocation of jobs and recording techniques can be found in the section entitled *Try It Yourself* on page 128. You may at this stage find it necessary to modify your plans. Allowances should be made for problems and opportunities which arise in rehearsal. If a scene does not work within two takes, rethink your approach, and try to keep to your schedule.

Move on to the next section. Rotate jobs between sections so that everyone experiences a variety of roles.

Afterwards

Watch your own video and share your immediate reactions to it.

For homework

Write an account of your activities during the day, paying attention to the following points:

- What did you find interesting, surprising and frustrating about the experience?
- Which parts of the video were the most successful – and why?
- Review your own attitude towards the exercise and what you may have learnt from it.
- On reflection, what might you do differently another time?

Later

Show your video to its intended audience. Your teacher will suggest the best person to help you with the arrangements. The audience's reactions and questions will tell you how successful you have been.

PART TWO
Facing the Facts

A News Story in the Making

Each evening, the news programme *Scotland Today* presents the day's news to an audience throughout Scotland in its six o'clock bulletin. Work on the stories begins early in the morning, though research may have begun days in advance. Here is an account of one news report which was produced on 24 February, 1988.

Early morning: Jon Kean is already at work scanning the early editions of the newspapers. As news editor, he is responsible for identifying news stories and organising reporters to cover them. Today will see protests by hospital staff against the planned privatisation of cleaning and catering services. Many hospital staff expect to lose their jobs when these services are handed over to private companies, and demonstrations are planned across Scotland. The editor thinks this will make today's main story.

Reporter Alan Saunby will cover the Glasgow demonstration and its impact on hospitals during the day. He will also conduct an interview with the hospital management. He discusses with the editor how he will tackle the story and what facilities he will need. His report will be just part of the news item.

Before the demonstration, Alan has to prepare his commentary and interview questions. After shooting all the pictures he will need, he will only have limited time to edit the material for transmission at 6 o'clock. Careful planning at this stage is necessary to avoid last-minute problems, but it leaves little room for manoeuvre.

The morning news conference. The producer announces the items to be covered and allocates tasks to members of the news team. Today, the hospital demonstration will be the first item in the bulletin.

FACING THE FACTS

The crew sets off. Alan takes with him a camera operator using a lightweight hand-held electronic camera (an ENG camera) and a sound recordist with his microphone. Their recording is stored on the videotape carried by the sound recordist.

The demonstration begins the march to Glasgow's George Square, headed by leading figures from the trade union movement and flanked by mounted police. The camera operator composes shots which will suggest the size, atmosphere and nature of the demonstration.

The crew moves ahead into the square and sets up in front of the bus from which the speakers will address the rally. As they speak, Alan makes a note of key moments to include in the report.

3 pm. Alan records an interview with Laurence Peterken, who leads the Glasgow Health Board. He gives the management's reactions to the day's demonstration.

Back at the studios, Alan reviews his material with a video editor and selects which moments to use in the report. The editor assembles the chosen pictures into a short sequence.

6 pm. On air. Newscaster Angus Simpson begins the broadcast. Alan's report is being watched by several million people throughout Scotland. It lasts just 3 minutes and 55 seconds.

Reporting the News

The partial picture

People sometimes make the mistake of thinking the camera cannot lie, that it does not influence the news but merely passes it on. But events and interviews featured in the news have been selected and arranged. The moment the operator aims the camera, a choice has already been made about what we may see and what we may not. We cannot know what the news team missed, ignored or edited out later.

Consider, for example, this picture which has been cropped so that you see just part of it. Photocopy this page and sketch in what you imagine to occupy the blank space:

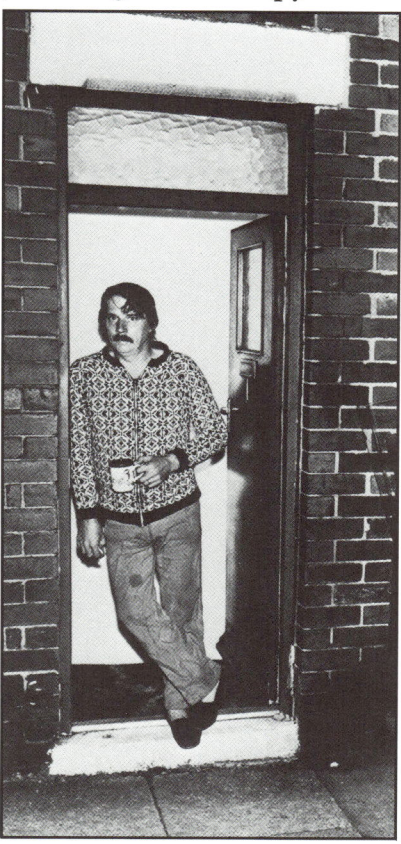

Compare your sketch with the actual picture on page 54.

- Does the new information change the way you interpret the original picture?
- What implications do your findings have for pictures in the news?

The television screen frames each picture and focuses our attention in a particular direction. It is a particular shape – more box-like than a cinema screen and with rounded edges. We view it in close-up. It is a medium which works particularly well with details and faces, but is not so good for large outdoor scenes. The shape and size of a cinema screen make it better for presenting panoramic shots.

CONSTRUCTING TELEVISION

Take, for instance, these three shots seen through a television shaped box:

- Give each picture a title.
- Now turn to the composite picture on page 54 and give it a title.

- The composite picture is more than the sum of its parts: it has a meaning of its own. How does seeing the entire picture affect your interpretation of the individual parts of it?
- How would you represent the larger beach scene on television? Imagine the people moving and talking, and consider how you would communicate the whole scene, given the limited size of the screen.
- Take a sheet of paper and cut out a television-shaped box, 4 cm wide and 3 cm deep. Hold it at hand's length in front of your eyes, and look at your surroundings through the frame.
- Keep the frame in front of your eyes for a minute or so, and try doing things you usually do — talk to someone, look out of the window, study the noticeboards, etc.
- In what ways does the frame limit and inhibit your usual view of the world?
- What did you find frustrating or revealing about this experience?

Another factor which influences the way we interpret pictures is the commentary of the reporter. This sometimes takes the form of a 'voice-over', so that we hear the reporter's explanation while we see the pictures.

Try watching five minutes of a news bulletin with the volume control turned right down. Imagine the accompanying commentary. Then listen to the same five minutes with the commentary turned up.

- Say what you notice about:

    — the appropriateness of the accompanying news pictures
    — the accuracy of the commentary on the news pictures
    — how much is obvious from pictures alone

Practical considerations

News services realise that they cannot report every detail and that there are important limitations on the reporting of news.

There are a number of practical considerations:

— *Time* is short.
— There is the *cost* to consider.
— Suitable well-informed *reporters* must be available.
— *Other news*, possibly more important, is competing for attention.
— *Ease of reporting* is a consideration. Some stories are easier to report than others — good pictures, clear issues and willing interviewees make life simpler.
— All stories must be *researched and checked* for accuracy. Politically sensitive issues must be reported with care.

Consider the practical problems which confront the news team when the following stories arise:

> 1 A shock assassination in Latin America.
> 2 An explosion on a North Sea oil rig.
> 3 A military build-up in a province of a middle-eastern country.
> 4 Developments on the Japanese stock exchange which have complex implications for Britain.
> 5 The Princess Royal visits Southfork Ranch in Dallas.
> 6 Death of a much-loved film star in California.
> 7 War games in progress in the Orkneys.
> 8 A near miss of aircraft over Heathrow.
> 9 A scandal concerning the private life of a Government minister.

- Jot down a list of practical considerations which face the news team in deciding whether to pursue each story.
- Note any additional information you would require before proceeding.
- There is room for only five stories in the bulletin. Decide which ones to report and justify your choice.

Time constraints

The news team works against deadlines, not only to identify and collect the news, but also to prepare it for broadcast. This may involve writing a voice-over and editing material to fit the time slot. A late item poses more problems because there isn't much time to polish the story. One solution is to prepare the story angle or outline in advance, in order to cut down delays at a later stage, but this doesn't leave a lot of room for unexpected twists. On the whole, reporters don't wait for news to happen: stories have to be sought, interviews have to be booked and background information has to be researched. These things take time. So a lot of thought goes into advance planning.

Planned events such as demonstrations, conferences and publicity stunts are organised in advance. The news team has time to prepare for them. The organisers are also aware of the news value of their events: they may well arrange press releases, camera positions and keynote speeches specifically designed for the television news. It is now quite common for politicians to release key statements shortly before big news deadlines. Knowing the time constraints, they anticipate that a pithy statement will be taken unedited by the news service. Thus they have more direct control over the substance of the broadcast.

Nonetheless, many newsworthy items break without warning, and the news team is called upon to construct reports at short notice. Even routine events such as demonstrations and parliamentary debates develop in unexpected ways. No news story can be completely predicted. Under these circumstances, the reporter must be alert to new story angles as they emerge, and be prepared to pursue them.

FACING THE FACTS

- What different time constraints are imposed by events such as:
    - a shipping disaster
    - a surprise offensive in part of a long-running war
    - a leader's speech at a party political conference
    - the summarising speeches of an important Parliamentary debate
    - news from Australia
    - the winning goal at the cup final

Gathering domestic news in the United Kingdom is relatively easy compared with a large country like America, which straddles several time zones. Events happen in New York while San Francisco is still asleep. Indeed, the invention of the videotape recorder was prompted by the need to transmit programmes at local times throughout America. Our own news service still faces time zone problems in reporting foreign affairs, and also in live 'link-ups' across the continents.

Competing news

One of the problems faced by the news service is the fixed timing of the bulletin. Not only must it go out at the same hour each day, but it must occupy the same length of time. A day packed with incident may be interesting, but the stories have to be short if everything is to get attention. Some stories may be elbowed out for more important items. Take these two stories:

The first day of discussion in Parliament about a law to increase the upper speed limit on motorways to 80 mph
Material prepared: commentary from reporter on the spot, summing up the debate
highlights of the speeches for and against
interviews with police, RAC and AA
vox pops (several mini-interviews) with motorists
an illustrated history of speed restrictions

Armed robbery in Carlisle
Security van attacked in broad daylight, witnessed by shoppers. Injuries serious, but not fatal. Security guards ousted from the van and left in road as the three masked robbers sped off.

Material available: interviews with eye witnesses
hospital spokesperson commenting on condition of guards
snaps taken by shopper as the event occurred
interview with detective in charge of investigation
recent material about similar robberies in the area

- Both of these stories are particularly well-resourced. The material is varied and unusual. Most news editors would want to find time for them in their news bulletin. But time is limited, and the bulletin is just 15 minutes long.

- In a group, discuss what you would do if those two stories came up on the same day as the following items:

> A shooting in Northern Ireland
> The Royal Barbeque – honours Britain's stars of stage and screen
> Near air disaster in Heathrow's crowded skies
> Train derailment – only minor injuries
> First day of the TUC Conference
> General election day in Italy
> Unemployment figures for this month

- Make a list showing:
    - which stories you would include in the bulletin
    - the running order
    - how many minutes on each story

- Now discuss how you would deal with the two stories if they came up on the same day as these items:

> Motorway pile-up – three cars – one person dead
> American President resigns
> Triplets born on Isle of Wight
> State visit by European prime minister
> Unexpected bonanza in fishing harvest
> Freak winds in Cornwall
> Large motor company pulls out of Britain – thousands of redundancies expected

- Compare the length and position of the two stories in each case, and justify your decisions.
- List the factors you took into account each time in ordering and timing the whole bulletin.
- Put these factors into order of importance.

A story which appears half way through the news might, on a slack day, have been the second item. On a busy day, it might have been squeezed near the end. News stories are tailored to fit the overall news pattern of the day.

Setting the agenda

The news team decides what to report and what not to report, so to a large extent it controls public awareness. Events which are kept out of the news don't bother us because we never hear about them.

The way events are reported also influences our own viewpoint. Take interviews, for example. A politician may be longing to explain the party's policy towards the health service, but the interviewer may not ask questions about it. On the other hand, the interviewer may push for a definite reply to a specific point which the politician cannot or will not answer.

The skill of the interviewer lies in asking questions which will prompt revealing answers on fundamental issues.

FACING THE FACTS

- What would be the three most searching questions you could put to the following people, in their professional capacity, in a public interview?
    - the Prime Minister
    - your headteacher
    - a person of your choice currently in the news
- Compare ideas and imagine how the interviewees would deal with the questions.
- Try recording an interview with a local personality, based on a list of well-researched questions.

Newscasting

Newscasters deliver the news in a distinctive manner.

- Imagine you are the newscaster.
    - What are you wearing?
    - How is your hair done?
    - Where are you sitting?
    - Where is the camera?
    - What is behind you?
- Read this aloud:

> Three people were rushed to Bristol Hospital today after a boating accident on the River Avon. The three teenagers, who were participating in a week of river sports organised by Riverfun Holidays, were injured when their boat capsized after striking an abandoned car on the river bed. Riverfun's Manager, Mr David Jones, said that the company regretted the accident, but was in no way to blame. He is demanding that the River Authority clears the river bed. He stressed that the injuries were minor and the teenagers were never in danger of drowning. They are said to be making a good recovery and will be released from hospital tomorrow.

- Discuss how you dealt with these matters in your reading:
    - the tone of delivery
    - the pace of delivery
    - eye contact with the camera/audience
    - starting and finishing the report
- Discuss why these conventions of reading and behaving have come about in newscasting.

Are there other ways of delivering the news? Consider these alternatives:

A guest opinion – different people are invited to read the news with their own comments and opinions.

No commentary, no newscasters – but the people involved in the news are invited to give their comments within a set time limit.

Group news – the news is delivered and discussed by a panel.

- How might the boating accident story be approached in these alternative bulletins?
- What effect would the changes have on other aspects of presentation, such as the tone, pace and look of the bulletin?
- How do you think audiences would react to alternative news bulletins?
- Make a list of newscasters and discuss which ones you prefer.
- What do newscasters have in common?
- What are their distinguishing features?
- Imagine you have to recruit a newscaster. Write a job advertisement outlining the kind of person you are looking for.

Complete photographs for 'The Partial Picture'

News as Narrative

One of the important functions of the news service is to convey information in a form that will be easy to digest. This is one reason why news is often presented as ongoing stories. Even so, some issues are hard to encapsulate in a few moments. A development on the stock market or a conflict between religious sects rarely receives a full explanation on the main news. These issues tend to be developed more in current affairs programmes.

Making stories of the news

The ITN news team

The vocabulary of news presentation admits to making stories out of events:

> 'tonight's main *story*'
> 'a real life *drama*'
> 'a *dramatic* new development'

The newscaster acts as a narrator or storyteller, and the news footage is like an illustration. Indeed, the first news stories had no live pictures at all. They were simply read aloud, over a still picture. Even after the appearance of newscasters in 1955, it was some years before live footage was used to illustrate the stories.

Notice the way that news 'headlines' preceding the bulletin tend to dramatise the events to be reported. For example, these headlines were broadcast in April 1988 on various channels. Study the wording:

News bulletin 1
Hello, good evening.

After last night's message to the Government over the poll tax in the Commons, a hint of more trouble today from the House of Lords. Even as the Government sets about repairing the damage wrought by its own backbenchers, Lord Jenkins of the Democrats prepares an amendment for debate in the Lords. And we hear the views on last night's vote of the former Government leader and deputy Prime Minister – Lord Whitelaw tells us that the vote was a setback for the Government but he expects the bill will get safely through the Lords.

The other headlines tonight:

– Voters in New York decide the fate of the Democratic presidential contenders – will they choose Jackson or Dukakis? – and can Albert Gore survive?

– Harland and Woolf clinches a £260 million deal to build the world's largest luxury liner.

– In the Gulf, after the noise and fury of yesterday's attack, both sides take stock, but British merchant ships are told to keep out.

– And ITN announces its plan to take its television news service into the nineties and beyond. More than a hundred jobs will go.

— Also tonight, a special report as Israel marks a significant anniversary. Forty years after its perilous founding, the nation remembers at a time when it still feels united by history, but torn by doubt and internal conflict.

News bulletin 2
— The leaked cabinet letter – Mrs Thatcher denies a double-cross, and accuses Mr Kinnock of receiving a stolen document.

— No proper apology from the Labour MP who threw the Mace on the floor. He's marched out of the Commons by his Party's deputy chief whip.

— The Royal Navy tells British ships to stay away from the Gulf as Iran says it will respond forcefully to American bullying.

— Teachers are offered a pay rise of four and a quarter per cent. A Union leader calls for a campaign of half day strikes.

— And the world's biggest cruise liner will be built in Belfast – if the government picks up £100 million of the bill.

News bulletin 3
— Mr Dukakis is ahead in New York and in the White House Race.

— British ships are told, 'Steer clear of the Gulf'.

— He wants his dream ship for £100 million from the taxpayer.

— Mr Ron Brown – *out* of the Commons, *in* Labour's bad books.

— And hope springs eternal on a bald man's head.

- Compare the language of the headlines.
- Compare the approach taken by each headline – what is the news 'angle'?
- Why do news bulletins use headlines?

Television thrives on action pictures. Our ears prick up at the promise of excitement, so news tends to dwell upon the immediate and the sensational. Negotiations are termed 'rows', industrial relations are not reported until direct confrontation provides dramatic pictures, and political debates are portrayed as battles between personalities.

This tradition of drama in news stories means that they concentrate on the symptoms of social strife, rather than the underlying causes. Consider the way one's attention is directed in the following stories by answering the questions that follow:

A sick baby cannot be treated because cuts in the health service have axed intensive care cots. Television coverage brings an unsolicited flood of public generosity to pay for a private operation.

A particularly brutal killing in Northern Ireland is reported at length on television. The scenes are shocking and explicit.

A report on shipyard redundancies shows one of the livelier moments on picket duty. There is an interview with a company representative in the board room, and an interview with workers on the picket line outside.

A group of MPs walks out of the House of Commons chamber as a protest over a point of principle about which they feel strongly. The main element of the report is an interview with their party leader, who is asked to comment on the action.

The proceedings of a big court case are followed on the television news. Cameras are not allowed in court, but the defendant is seen arriving each day, covered with a blanket. Proceedings are summarised by the reporter, with the aid of artists' sketches.

- Discuss the following points:
    - Which aspect of each story captures immediate attention?
    - What are the political issues raised by each story, though not necessarily highlighted in them?
    - What is the immediate effect of each report on the viewing public?
    - What are the long-term effects of each report on the people in the stories?
    - What alternative ways are there of reporting these stories?

Finding an honest way of reporting the news is not easy. The reporter has to gather together all sorts of random and sometimes conflicting information, and make some sense of it for the viewer.

Over the next few pages you will find the raw material for three news stories. Read them carefully and prepare each one for broadcast. This will mean deciding on an approach to the event, selecting the appropriate material to make a news story out of it, and writing the script for your news report. Prepare a 25–30 second report on each story indicating what you would show on screen. Afterwards, answer the questions that follow.

Story 1: A rare cottage is burnt down
Editor's memo pad:

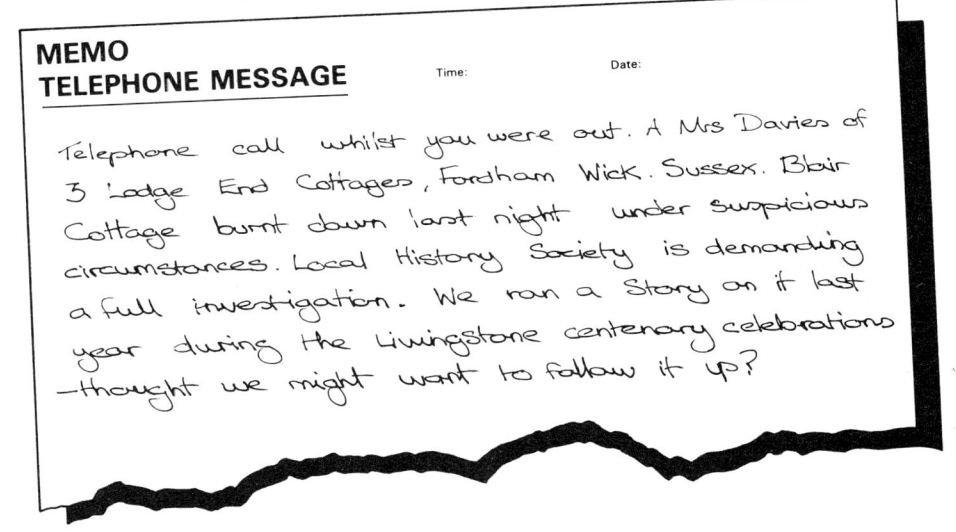

MEMO
TELEPHONE MESSAGE Time: Date:

Telephone call whilst you were out. A Mrs Davies of 3 Lodge End Cottages, Fordham Wick, Sussex. Blair Cottage burnt down last night under suspicious circumstances. Local History Society is demanding a full investigation. We ran a story on it last year during the Livingstone centenary celebrations — thought we might want to follow it up?

Telephone call to police:

Hello, this is Fordham Wick Duty Officer... Yes, we have been notified, the site was inspected this morning... No, we'd have to know a lot more before we could accuse anyone of arson... Yes, completely destroyed, beams have gone completely... a great shame I agree... No, it won't be worth it, there's nothing to save and the site had been sold off anyway... McGuire's Building Developments... No, all above board, the cottage was going to stay as a feature, there were no plans to demolish it, quite an attraction, I'd think, but pretty run down, you know, since the Centenary... Squatters in it up until recently, but they moved on a few weeks ago... Investigation? I don't think so, sir, it's too late, isn't it? It was rather dilapidated, sir, and now the beams have gone, they won't come back.

Extract from local history book, five years old:

BLAIR COTTAGE

Blair Cottage, built 1583, nestles on the outskirts of Fordham Wick and is visited by 500 sightseers each year. It is a typical rural cottage of Tudor times, but the only one remaining in this area of Sussex. Its attraction lies in the elaborate decorative carvings on its internal beams, said to have been carved by its first occupant, a cabinet maker and woodworker whose work can also be seen on the altar and pews of the parish church of St Eldred's in the neighbouring village of Poultney. Local legend has it that the ghost of the carver walks the cottage, admiring his carvings by the light of a lamp. Sightings of the ghost have increased in recent years. Its other famous occupant was the poet Livingstone who rented the cottage to write his *Dreamland* poems during 1880–1884. The Cottage was partly renovated 6 years ago by the Local History Society and opened to the public at weekends for a nominal charge.

FACING THE FACTS

Telephone call to Arthur Hamblin, president of Fordham Wick Local History Society:

> Yes, an absolutely tragic event, deliberate mischief I've no doubt... absolutely irreplaceable, I can't tell you how upset we are in the village... Yes, we've arranged a meeting with the Chief Constable over in Lorchester for tomorrow. Really, one can't let a major tragedy like this pass by without protest. We need to know how the fire started and what can be done; fires don't start themselves, someone's to blame... We've had squatters here recently, I wouldn't be surprised if... What? No, we didn't have the funds to run it ourselves, but the Conservancy Trust assured us they would maintain it, they can afford the restoration costs you know, thousands of pounds, we were told just to save the beams. We don't have that sort of money.

Reporter's notepad – interviews with local people:

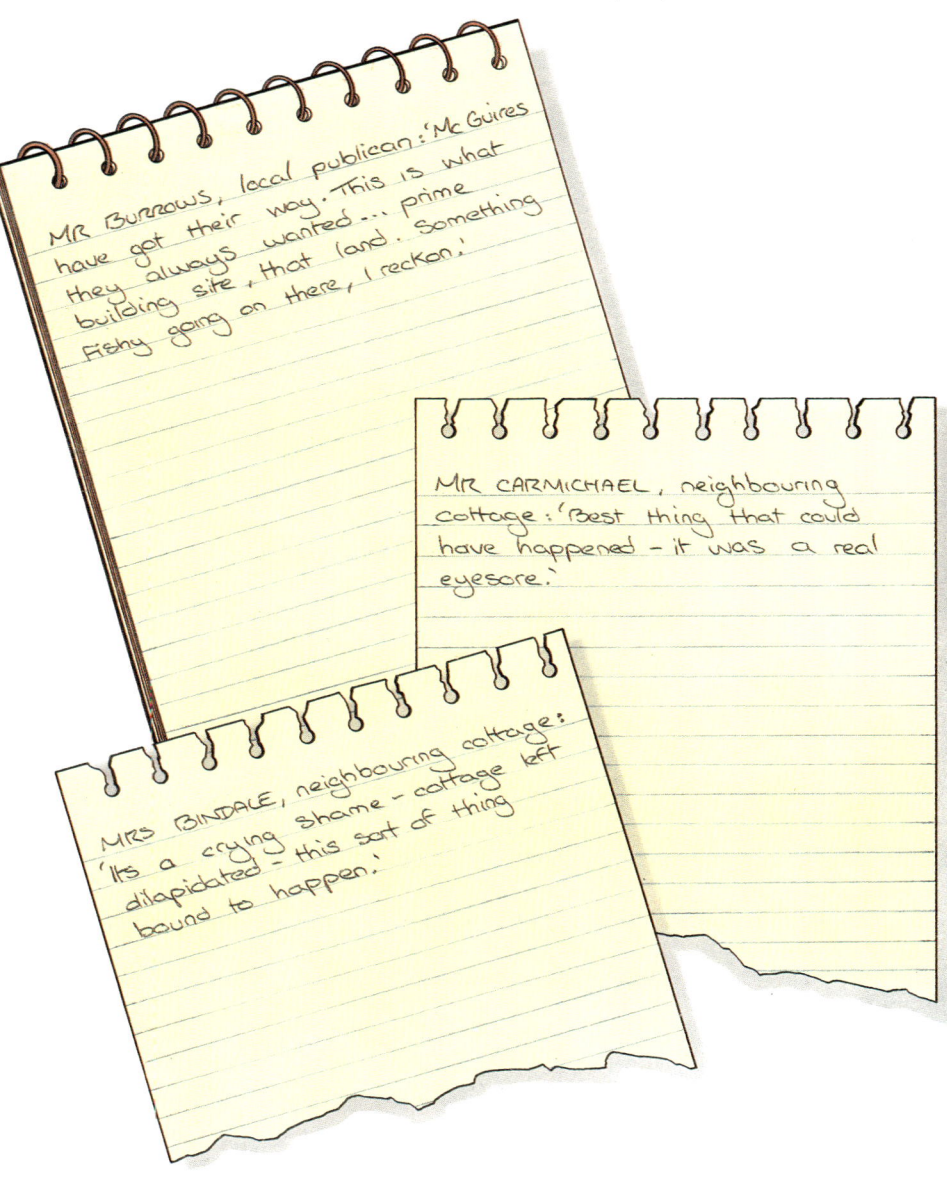

MR BURROWS, local publican: 'McGuires have got their way. This is what they always wanted... prime building site, that land. Something fishy going on there, I reckon.'

MR CARMICHAEL, neighbouring cottage: 'Best thing that could have happened – it was a real eyesore.'

MRS BINDALE, neighbouring cottage: 'It's a crying shame – cottage left dilapidated – this sort of thing bound to happen.'

McGuires Building Developments

press release

The company notes with regret the destruction of Blair Cottage. It proposes to name a road in the new development commemorating its existence.

The site surveyor will inspect the remains later this week and anything of value will be donated to the local history museum at Lorchester. It is likely that the land will be cleared for building development.

- When preparing your report for this story, assume that, although there will be no time to record video interviews, you can get pictures of the scene and archive material.

Story 2: Announced redundancies at Crown Motor Company

FEDERATION OF CAR MANUFACTURING EMPLOYEES

PRESS STATEMENT

Management today unveiled plans for over 1000 redundancies at the Crown Motor Company's Codsthorpe plant. We will be calling a mass meeting for tomorrow morning to fight these draconian measures.

This announcement by the company is a slap in the face for the workforce, who have already endured cuts in staffing levels and worsening conditions of work over the past two years.

Management has displayed a cynical disregard for the national agreement of last year, in which it promised no further job cuts without full consultation. We will be taking legal advice over this deplorable action.

```
            CROWN MOTOR COMPANY
               PRESS RELEASE

Today the Crown Motor Company is presenting
a radical plan for the restructuring of its
operations at the Codsthorpe plant.  Today's
proposals are part of a long-term campaign for
increased efficiency and profitability which
will enable us to remain strong in the face of
increasing competition.

As part of our streamlining process it will be
necessary to change many outdated practices and
to slim down to a competitive size.  Management
hopes to implement job reductions voluntarily
where possible, but reserves the right to carry
out compulsory redundancies if necessary, in
order to meet its target of a minimum staff
reduction of 1000.

In a message to employees this morning, Plant
Director Barry Makedime announced: 'These
dynamic and constructive proposals are the first
step towards a bright future in Codsthorpe for
the Crown Motor Company.  By prompt action now
we can overcome our inefficiency, and emerge
leaner and fitter, to boldly face the challenge
of our rivals in the marketplace.  I sincerely
hope that the unions will join me in protecting
our future by accepting these plans today.'
```

'Vox pops' – interviews conducted with employees leaving the factory after yesterday's announcement:

Brian Harris, production line worker:
'Disgraceful. I've worked for Crown for 12 years and now I'm likely to lose my job. There's no chance of another job round here. I blame the government for it – they're encouraging companies to act like this. Yes, I'll be voting against the plans at tomorrow's meeting.'

Neville Thomas, accounts office:
'Well, the company has to become more efficient. No one likes redundancies, but there's far too much time-wasting down on the shop floor. I think the proposals are common sense.'

Jane Connors, secretary:
'I think everyone's rather depressed by the news. We don't know yet which departments are going to be most affected. I suppose we'll just have to wait and see. Well, I'm not sure which way I'll vote. The company seems to have made its mind up whatever we do.'

MEMO
TELEPHONE MESSAGE

Time: Date:

Phone call while you were out from Geoff Roper, Secretary of local Trades Council: Very disappointed at the news of redundancies. Will add to the job crisis locally — with recent closure of two other factories, unemployment in Codsthorpe is now over 20%. Called upon company to enter into dialogue with unions to find alternative approach, including possible job-sharing scheme. Shows the need for controls on foreign car imports, which are undermining our motor industry.

Share prices for Crown dropped again yesterday after the announcement of poor trading figures for the first six months of the year, with new car sales down 10% on last year's figures. There was a ray of hope for investors later in the day though, when Crown announced proposed discussions with a major Japanese company. No details have been released, but it is rumoured that Crown intends to buy Japanese engines and computer technology for its new range of cars due out next year.

Three months ago, from *Business Finance Weekly*

A CROWNING SUCCESS:

It's Official – workers at the Crown Motor Company are the tops, say their bosses!
Last week the assembly lines produced a whopping 10,000 new Crown Crackers, the sporty little hatchbacks that are proving so popular – and that's a record!
The proud assembly team were presented with badges and a commemorative wall plaque by Production Director, John Crockett. He told reporters, "Our adoption of new technology, coupled with improved quality control, is making us the market leader. We are very proud of this achievement, and look forward to the next record!"

Last year's *Codsthorpe Chronicle*

Crown Motor Company have won a £3.5 million contract to build a car plant in Brazil. Work is expected to commence in the coming month. Director of Corporate Affairs Michael McChide hailed the contract as a major triumph for the British motor industry, which he said had proved it could beat off foreign competition to clinch the deal.

Last week's *National Reporter*

Story 3: Parliament debate banning smoking in all public buildings

THE RIGHT HONOURABLE MEMBER FOR RIFFIELD NORTH: (*continued*) ... inevitable job losses in the tobacco industry. In my constituency, for example, a total of 1,200 workers are employed in cigarette manufacture. This measure would have devastating effects on them and on the wider economy of the Driffield region. I urge members to vote against this ill-conceived motion.

SPEAKER: I call the Right Honourable Member for Partington.

THE RIGHT HONOURABLE MEMBER FOR PARTINGTON: Mr Speaker, the Right Honourable Member for Driffield North has blown a smokescreen over (*laughter*) ... a smokescreen over the real issues of this debate. May I remind the House of the points raised so forcefully earlier in the debate: namely, the link between smoking and fatal diseases; the pollution caused by smoky atmospheres; the destruction of huge areas of forest by rapacious companies and the corruption of innocent lungs by parents who smoke in the presence of their children, thereby forcing them to inhale the killer fumes? Is it therefore not time to ban cigarettes not only from our libraries, town halls and offices, but from this House as well?

(*Cries and guffaws; some chesty coughing*)

SPEAKER: I call the Right Honourable Member for Stoke Tenton.

THE RIGHT HONOURABLE MEMBER FOR STOKE TENTON: I have the advantage of many years' experience in the manufacture of cigarettes, and I have read with interest the various reports purporting to link cigarettes with fatal diseases. It is my opinion that each person has the right to make up their own minds about the evidence, and to smoke when and where ...

(*Interruptions: 'Shame, shame...'; 'Vested interests'; 'Murderer', etc.*)

THE RIGHT HONOURABLE MEMBER FOR STOKE TENTON: If I may continue ...

(*further interruptions*)

SPEAKER: Order, order ... if the House does not restrain itself I will be obliged to suspend unruly members ...

- What was the main thrust of each story – the main angle, if you like – and how did you decide on it?
- Read aloud two or three different versions of each story and discuss the use each one makes of similar material.
- Go back and highlight the material you did not incorporate in your report, and justify each omission.
- Make a list of factors used to select and reject material (for example, relevance, balance).

The cult of personalities

Each story has its stars, and many of them become famous television personalities. Can you remember the events which made these people household names?

- Cynthia Payne
- Eddie the Eagle
- Zola Budd and Mary Decker
- Terry Waite

There are personalities who become so famous that they themselves become a running news story. What events can you associate with these favourites?

- Ian Botham
- James Anderton
- Richard Branson
- Frank Bruno

The media also has its anti-heroes. Politicians are particularly vulnerable, especially if their views are non-conformist. There have been several bogeymen and bogeywomen in recent years. What do you know from television about:

- Arthur Scargill
- The Bishop of Durham
- Edwina Currie
- Tony Benn

Television treats such people with a disrespect they may not deserve, but their public image has been fixed. Audiences rather enjoy having scapegoats and clowns. Though all politicians make incautious remarks, they are not always reported with the same relish reserved for these anti-heroes.

- Can you name people who have achieved fame or notoriety in the news recently?
- Were they people whose names were known to you already?
- What is it they have said or done which is so remarkable?
- Can you see any bias in the way famous politicians are represented on television?
- Can you see any bias in the way specific groups in society are referred to, for example:

    - the loony left
    - the Tory wets
    - yuppies

The royal family are favourite news personalities.

- What personalities have been built up around each member of the royal family?
- Recall recent news stories about the things they have said or done. Would these incidents have been noteworthy coming from other people?
- Why do the royal family merit attention in the news?

Newsworthiness

As we have seen, practical considerations have an enormous influence on what appears in the television news. The medium of television copes well with news which is visual, dramatic and immediate. And it also uses the facial close up to good effect in eyewitness accounts and face-to-face interviews. Other news media are effective in different areas. Print is a much better medium for detailed analysis, for example, because it gives the reader time for reflection. Television has great impact, but it sets its own pace.

Below is a news story that was reported in July 1988, in a newspaper and a television bulletin:

1 Newspaper

Doctors will vigorously resist attempts by the Government to force them to follow other professions in advertising their services, the chairman of the British Medical Association's council warned yesterday. Dr John Marks told the Association's meeting in Norwich: 'Advertising can never be in the best interests of patients, even if it were in the best interests of some doctors. It is self-aggrandisement and gilding the lily.

'Experience shows that those who write the best advertisements are not necessarily the best doctors,' he said. There were those around who would exploit the vulnerability of the sick by promising the unobtainable. Doctors were in favour of giving patients more information about their services to help them choose a doctor. But there was 'a world of difference between that and advertising'.

The doctors' refusal to permit advertising has been referred to the Monopolies and Mergers Commission.

2 Television

The opening shot shows the conference. The sound is the newscaster's voice-over:
At the BMA Annual Conference, doctors have rejected Government proposals to allow doctors to advertise their services.

The picture cuts to a speaker addressing the conference:
'What fun we could have. Adverts in the press. Local papers for the GPs, national press for the consultants (*laughter*). Tiny little squares to start with for the physicians – "Cut price check-ups for cash!" – "ECGs on satin paper!" – "If you have no symptoms, come anyway; our computer will give you some suggestions!"' (*laughter and applause*)

The picture cuts to a wide angle shot of the conference again, and the presenter voices over:
The doctors deny their opposition to advertising is designed to protect doctors. They claim it's the patients' interests that must come first.

- What differences do you notice in the treatment of the story in each case?
- What are the particular strengths of each medium?

- What are the limitations of each medium?
- What practical considerations have dictated the content and approach of the television bulletin?

News values

With so many events happening in one day, a way must be found of judging which ones merit attention. It is the job of the news editor to make this judgement. The choice and order of stories is neither natural nor obvious. The editor compiles the bulletin with quite specific priorities in mind. By now, we are all so used to these priorities that they seem natural.

How easy is it to identify the main stories, and put them in order of priority? Read through the items below, all of which occurred on Thursday 28 April, 1988 and compile a running order for the evening news lasting 30 minutes, showing the order and length of each item.

1 *Afghanistan*
Pictures from Afghanistan: refugees move back as the Russian army withdraws.

2 *Death of a Peer*
The great campaigner, Lord Brockway, dies this evening, aged 99. Several archive pictures.

3 *Polish Strike*
First Polish strike for seven years. Strikes illegal. Steelworkers demanding higher wages in face of rapid rise in cost of living. Pictures of town available.

4 *Share Index News*
Update on share index figures.

5 *Ken Livingstone*
Ken Livingstone is the only MP to be denied an office in the House of Commons. He decides to work from home, visiting Parliament for key debates only. Interview.

6 *French Election*
Today's activities in the run-up to the French Presidential election, heightened by anti-French riots in New Caledonia, a French colony. Pictures of riots and pre-election TV debate.

7 *Local Elections*
Review of party campaigns in run-up to next week's local elections. Particularly busy activity in Wolverhampton, a marginal region. Pictures of visiting political figures.

8 *Cricket Results*

9 *Heart Transplant Baby*
First birthday celebrations of the youngest ever heart-transplant patient. Pictures of her birthday visit to the hospital where the operation took place.

10 *Queen in Australia*
Pictures of the Queen's engagements in Australia.

11 *Panama*
The Americans say they are satisfied that the unpopular President has agreed to stand down.

12 *Nuclear Test Victims*
Soldiers who were used as guinea pigs in the first nuclear tests in 1953 have won a court ruling to take the Government to court, to ask for compensation for illnesses they say arise from exposure to radiation. Archive material and interviews with victims and medical experts available.

13 *ICI*
ICI profits are up to £385 million this year, and a new director has been appointed.

14 *Gibraltar Programme*
Despite Government protests, the Independent Broadcasting Authority has allowed ITV to broadcast a politically sensitive programme about the shooting of IRA members in Gibraltar. Extracts from the programme available.

15 *Racing*
Results from the first flat race of the season.

16 *Ferry Dispute*
Developments in the ferry dispute. Union support grows for the P & O strikers. Strikebreakers hired to sail the ships. Local bad feeling. Interviews with pickets and management.

17 *USA/Canada Summit*
Talks between USA and Canada. USA encourages Canada to buy British built submarines.

18 *European Cancer Week*
The start of a Europe-wide campaign to inform people about measures they can take to prevent cancer. A report on cures and treatments which are increasingly successful, especially amongst children.

- Write up the order and timing of your 30-minute bulletin.
- How did you decide which items were more important than others? Make a list of all the factors you took into account and list them in order of priority.

Compare your bulletin with the evening news broadcasts for that day, which are given on the next page.

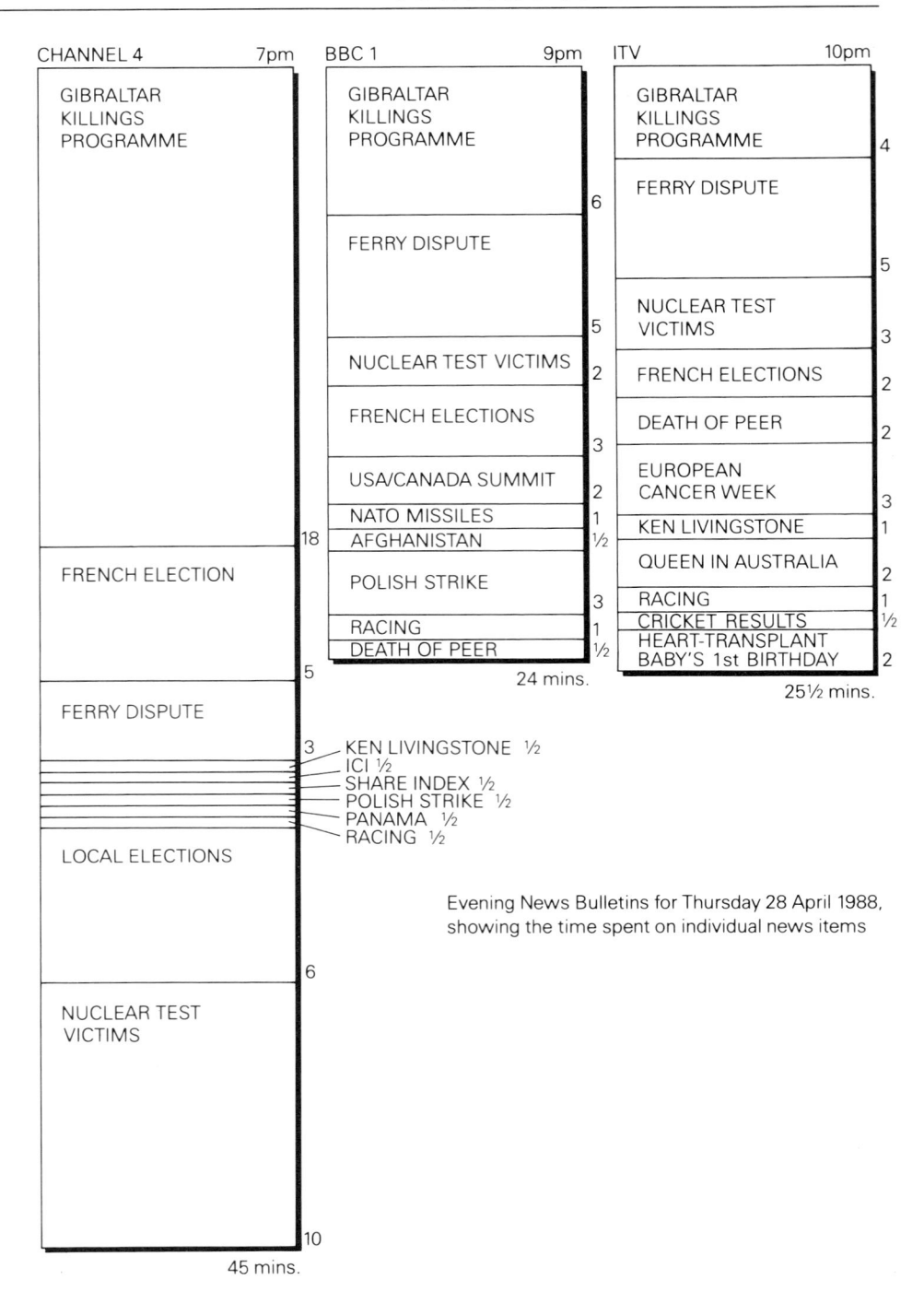

```
CHANNEL 4        7pm    BBC 1           9pm    ITV             10pm
┌─────────────────┐     ┌─────────────────┐    ┌─────────────────┐
│ GIBRALTAR       │     │ GIBRALTAR       │    │ GIBRALTAR       │ 4
│ KILLINGS        │     │ KILLINGS        │    │ KILLINGS        │
│ PROGRAMME       │     │ PROGRAMME       │    │ PROGRAMME       │
│                 │     │                 │ 6  ├─────────────────┤
│                 │     │                 │    │ FERRY DISPUTE   │
│                 │     ├─────────────────┤    │                 │ 5
│                 │     │ FERRY DISPUTE   │    ├─────────────────┤
│                 │     │                 │    │ NUCLEAR TEST    │
│                 │     │                 │ 5  │ VICTIMS         │ 3
│                 │     ├─────────────────┤    ├─────────────────┤
│                 │     │ NUCLEAR TEST    │ 2  │ FRENCH ELECTIONS│ 2
│                 │     │ VICTIMS         │    ├─────────────────┤
│                 │     ├─────────────────┤    │ DEATH OF PEER   │ 2
│                 │     │ FRENCH ELECTIONS│ 3  ├─────────────────┤
│                 │     ├─────────────────┤    │ EUROPEAN        │ 3
│                 │     │ USA/CANADA SUMMIT│ 2 │ CANCER WEEK     │
│                 │     ├─────────────────┤    ├─────────────────┤
│                 │  18 │ NATO MISSILES   │ 1  │ KEN LIVINGSTONE │ 1
│                 │     │ AFGHANISTAN     │ ½  ├─────────────────┤
├─────────────────┤     │ POLISH STRIKE   │    │ QUEEN IN AUSTRALIA│ 2
│ FRENCH ELECTION │     │                 │ 3  │ RACING          │ 1
│                 │     ├─────────────────┤    │ CRICKET RESULTS │ ½
│                 │     │ RACING          │ 1  │ HEART-TRANSPLANT│
│                 │     │ DEATH OF PEER   │ ½  │ BABY'S 1st BIRTHDAY│ 2
│                 │  5                           25½ mins.
├─────────────────┤         24 mins.
│ FERRY DISPUTE   │     3 ─ KEN LIVINGSTONE ½
│                 │       ─ ICI ½
│                 │       ─ SHARE INDEX ½
│                 │       ─ POLISH STRIKE ½
│                 │       ─ PANAMA ½
│                 │       ─ RACING ½
├─────────────────┤
│ LOCAL ELECTIONS │     Evening News Bulletins for Thursday 28 April 1988,
│                 │     showing the time spent on individual news items
│                 │  6
├─────────────────┤
│ NUCLEAR TEST    │
│ VICTIMS         │
│                 │
│                 │
│                 │
│                 │
└─────────────────┘ 10
      45 mins.
```

Since the news bulletins each last a different length of time, it is interesting to compare the percentage of time each one spent on the items:

Percentage of bulletin time spent on the major stories

	Channel 4	BBC 1	ITV
Gibraltar	40%	25%	16%
Ferry dispute	7%	21%	20%
French election	11%	12%	8%
Nuclear victims	22%	8%	12%

- Compare the news bulletins above, considering these points:
    - which items were included or omitted
    - differences in the order of priority
    - the amount of real time spent on each item (in the first diagram)
    - the proportion of time spent on each item (in the second diagram)
    - the possible reasons for these choices

It is interesting to note that although news programmes see themselves as factual, they nonetheless differ in their approach and style. We are familiar with the idea of newspapers which appeal to different audiences – we speak of the 'tabloid' and 'quality' press – but does an equivalent exist in television news audiences? Certainly the notional audience changes, depending on the time of day and the length of the broadcast. A longer bulletin, such as the 50-minute Channel 4 evening news, aims for an audience seeking more in-depth reporting, with time to cover a wider range of issues.

- Reconsider the news headlines on pages 55–6 and discuss what they reveal about the supposed audience for each news service. You may also like to consider the statistics given in the previous exercise, as a way of comparing different approaches.

A question of balance

We commonly expect news to give us a balanced view of events, by representing each point of view as fairly as possible. But this is not always easy to achieve.

Consider the news report illustrated in *A News Story In The Making*, which opens this section of the book. The report is about a demonstration by Health Service workers against the planned privatisation of hospital ancillary services such as cleaning and catering, which they believe would result in many redundancies and poorer services.

Before reading the transcript of that report on the next page, consider the issues at stake from the point of view of different people involved. What would be the main issues at stake for:

- an ancillary worker in a hospital
- a nurse
- a patient
- a hospital manager
- a viewer like yourself, not directly involved

Consider what perception each of these people have of:

- what has caused the demonstration
- the political principles at stake
- the day's events
- the aftermath of the demonstration and the long-term prospects

- In your opinion, what aspects of this story should receive most attention and why?
- Now read the transcript of the Glasgow report and reflect how far it satisfies your own expectations and how it might appear to the groups of people mentioned above:

ANGUS SIMPSON, NEWSCASTER: Good evening. Tens of thousands of Scottish health workers have taken to the streets in the biggest day of industrial action for years. They're protesting at plans to privatise parts of the Health Service. The unions say 6,000 health workers were out today, their numbers swelled by thousands of other workers including miners, local government employees and shipyard workers. 580 operations had to be cancelled, some of which will take months to reschedule. The unions have called today a triumph far exceeding their expectations, but Scottish Health Minister, Michael Forsyth, says he's disgusted that emergency cover was not being provided at some hospitals. Our industrial correspondent, Alan Saunby, has the first of our reports.

ALAN SAUNBY, REPORTER: The day of protest began with pickets outside all major hospitals in Glasgow. 200 non-essential operations were cancelled and only emergency patients were admitted. Over 5,000 ancillary staff stayed away. At the city's Western Infirmary, emergency cover was cut after two staff crossed picket lines.

STEVE TAYLOR, SHOP STEWARD: We're withdrawing one or two not so essential personnel. The effect of taking out the people we have done, who were there on emergency cover this morning, will have no detrimental effect to patient care whatsoever.

ALAN SAUNBY: Off-duty COHSE and NUPE nurses, and members of the Royal College were there to give their support.

UNIDENTIFIED NURSE: We're just wanting to show that we protest against the privatisation of the National Health Service and this is our way of saying, Look, we support the workers in the hospital in what they're doing today and we want to say that we're with them all the way, but unfortunately, you know, we just don't want to strike.

ALAN SAUNBY: There was a row when some domestic staff walked out at Yorkhill Sick Children's Hospital, and the Greater Glasgow Health Board claimed that broke the TUC's guidelines.

DOUGLAS MACINTYRE, SHOP STEWARD: That's certainly not the case. It does say that there should be a high dependency on children's hospitals, but it certainly doesn't exempt children's hospitals.

ALAN SAUNBY: The Duke Street Psychiatric Hospital in Glasgow, with 170 geriatric and dependent patients, was the worst hit. Only essential cleaning and catering could be done. Staff say it's going to be a long 24 hours. Union representatives tried to persuade their members to give emergency cover.

STEPHEN BLACK, HOSPITAL ADMINISTRATOR: The trade unions actually came to us and said, 'We have tried to get you essential cover but unfortunately that hasn't been the case. Staff feeling has been very

FACING THE FACTS

high and you haven't got anything.' So today we are finding that a basic management service is covering most of the major tasks in the hospital.

ALAN SAUNBY: Twenty catering staff normally work in the kitchen. One senior manager was left to provide hundreds of meals.

LAURENCE PETERKEN, GREATER GLASGOW HEALTH BOARD: The TUC guidelines specifically say that the elderly, children and mentally handicapped should be excluded, and I think it's quite disgraceful that a whole block of ancillary workers go out without leaving any cover at all.

ALAN SAUNBY: 25,000 demonstrators, including workers from shipyards and factories across Strathclyde, joined in the protest march, bringing the centre of Glasgow to a halt.

CAMPBELL CHRISTIE, SCOTTISH TRADES UNION CONGRESS (addressing the rally): We're here to support you in standing against this iniquitous effort to cut your conditions of service and to bring in private contractors on conditions that no reasonable workers would accept.

ALAN SAUNBY: Ironically, a tiny group called PULSE in favour of competitive tendering, held a counter-demonstration outside the STUC Offices in Glasgow.

LAURENCE PETERKEN, GREATER GLASGOW HEALTH BOARD: Competitive tendering is one way of making quite sure we don't have too many people in the kitchen when we don't have enough nurses on the wards.

ALAN SAUNBY: How soon will you be pressing ahead with the next step?

LAURENCE PETERKEN: We shall be announcing very shortly the catering contracts and we shall be interviewing Management Consultancy firms next week to choose those firms we're going to use to help coach our in-house tender teams, to make sure they've got an absolutely first-class chance of winning the tenders.

ALAN SAUNBY: The day of action was the climax of a wave of industrial demonstrations. Up to now the health unions, despite their anger and frustration, have worked hard to protect the patients, but both sides are still on a collision course.

- How fairly does the report reflect the concerns of the people involved, as you defined them in the opening exercise?
- What aspects of the story do you consider to be well-covered and what aspects are understated? Can you account for the particular emphases of the story?
- How 'balanced' is the report, and on what basis do you assess 'balance'?
- Re-edit the story using the material above to present a briefer news report of about one quarter the length, noting how you select and arrange the material to achieve your own notion of 'balance'.

You will realise that balance is not achieved simply by allotting equal time to each side, but is built into the approach of the report. It is interesting to note that neither the unions nor the management felt flattered by the report above:

> My initial reaction, watching the Glasgow film, was that it was heavily biased against the trade union position, because it emphasises the alleged lack of patient care and the like. And the interviews with Mr Peterken were indoors, and it's more easy to present your case, than the trade union officials who were on the picket line and having to do it in the context of outside, which I think is always a disadvantage. But then as the programme went on, the balance seemed to even up.
> **Campbell Christie,**
> **General Secretary of the Scottish Trade Union Congress**

> Well, I think it's slightly balanced in favour of the union. I was just trying to analyse the number of interviews, as it were, on each side of the equation and, er, it seemed there were about six interviews with people from the union point of view and four from what you might call the management point of view, and when you add that to the fact that the TUC was given the final word as well, I think that does give you a slight imbalance.
> **Laurence Peterken, General Manager, Glasgow Health Board**

Predictably perhaps, both sides felt that the report favoured the other. But this must not be seen as proof that the report was balanced or objective. The true test of balance is the impression taken away by viewers. There may be a great deal of information and comment from both sides of a dispute, but it's the attitude of the report which counts – the unspoken acts of bias contained in its approach.

For the news team, striving to give a truly balanced report presents certain dilemmas. Consider the following cases:

1 Did British television have a responsibility to explain the case of Argentina in the Falklands War?

2 How fair is it to concentrate on the internal discussions of a political party? For example, there was a much publicised division in the Conservative party over the introduction of the Poll Tax, and there have been divisions in the Labour party over nuclear disarmament. Consider how the reporting of these debates treats:

– other points of view entirely
– the function of political debate within parties
– the underlying issues of the discussion

3 On the issue of economic policy, each political party has a different stance. How much responsibility does television have to report the views of smaller parties, and how would it do this?

4 On the issue of nuclear weapons, the two main parties have very different opinions. How does television news strive to maintain a balance, and does this encourage people to 'sit in the middle'?

A news story which reports both sides of a conflict might not give them equal impact. The presentation may be quite different. Consider in detail the language of this news report broadcast on 24 March, 1988 on *News At Ten* (ITV), paying particular attention to the underlined words and those in bold (heavy print):

> *The item starts with the presenter speaking to camera:*
>
> Iran and Iraq have launched missile attacks on each other's capitals today, killing dozens of civilians and injuring hundreds more.
>
> *Cut to map of region:*
>
> Since **the so-called war of the cities** started again last month, Iraq has fired at least a hundred rockets at Iran, mainly at Tehran. Iran says six hundred Iranians have been killed and thirteen hundred injured. Iran has fired more than fifty missiles at Baghdad and other cities in Iraq.
>
> *Mix to Iraqi Television pictures of bomb damage in Baghdad, the capital of Iraq:*
>
> Iraqi Television showed pictures of today's damage in Baghdad – a children's hospital wrecked, they said, with nine dead and sixty injured. Houses were also bombed with more dead and injured. Iraq says it will keep up the air attacks until Iran agrees to a ceasefire. The Iranians say Tehran is being destroyed piece by piece.
>
> *Mix to a panoramic shot of Tehran, the capital of Iran, with the reporter in the foreground. Sound of siren:*
>
> <u>The howl of another air raid siren</u> brings Tehran to a virtual standstill. It means that <u>in just four minutes</u> time an Iraqi missile will strike, <u>wreaking more death and destruction</u> in the war of the cities.
>
> *Cut to pictures of Tehran streets, underground shelters, and hotel lobby:*
>
> Many people have already <u>fled the capital in fear.</u> Others now lead new lives in underground shelters. Deep below city centre apartment blocks, families have formed <u>subterranean ghettos</u> for protection and company during the <u>long hours of anxiety.</u> There's no comfort or privacy, and hardly any room for belongings, but some who've already lost homes, family and friends, have <u>precious little else in the world.</u> The wealthier Iranians can afford to pay for more luxurious shelter. They band together each evening in hotel lobbies to comfort each other between the many explosions <u>which send shudders through the capital.</u>
>
> *Still in Tehran, daytime shots of bomb damage. Sound of bombs followed by all-clear siren in background:*
>
> <u>The city holds its breath until the blasts are no more</u> and the all-clear is sounded. This hospital was hit in a recent attack; sixteen people were killed. But the raids are by no means one way; **it's a tit-for-tat cross country conflict** which, Iran is warning, could become far worse if it decides to deploy chemical weapons.

> *Cut to reporter speaking to camera:*
>
> The big fear now is that with the atrocity in Hallebja and this latest veiled threat from Iran, that the war of the cities could escalate into a chemical war.

- Consider the underlined words in the report. What impression is built up of the atmosphere in Iran from these words? By contrast, what impression are we given of the atmosphere in Iraq?
- What other differences do you notice in the presentation of the reports from the two capitals, and can you account for them?
- Consider the words in bold. What attitude do they invite the viewer to take towards the war?

The tone, emphasis and approach of a news report dictates its 'balance' as much as the proportion of time spent on individual items. Treatment is just as significant as time.

Editing the news

There is a limit to how much news can be broadcast in a bulletin. On a busy day, stories will be dropped or trimmed to fit the available space. The process of editing is significant because in selecting and trimming material, decisions have to be taken about what is and is not 'newsworthy'.

- Editing is therefore guided by certain values and priorities beyond the obvious practical constraints listed below. Try it yourself with the following script sent in by a foreign correspondent. As editor, it is your job to trim it down to half its present length, bearing in mind the following points:

  — There will be a newscaster available to make brief links between the different reports in the item.

  — Time is short, so your edits must be bold. It takes too long to remove a phrase here or there. Use only one or two cuts in any one section.

  — The end result must be clear and punchy. It must keep to the point and avoid confusing the viewers.

Sandy Gall – well-known for his news reports from Afghanistan

> For the third day running, Western journalists have been unable to travel outside the Government controlled areas in the Far Eastern state of Kaltrea. Tonight, rebel troops are surrounding the capital, Amchuta, after a day of heavy fighting in the south of Kaltrea, and the defending troops of President Sonchak are now staring defeat in the face. A strictly enforced curfew is in operation, and the atmosphere is extremely tense.
>
> In a radio broadcast this afternoon, a Government spokesman appealed for calm, claiming: *'Our troops are holding firm against the enemy attack. They have the overwhelming support of the Kaltrean nation, whose future freedom and prosperity depends on the defeat of the terrorists.'* A reliable source close to the rebel leadership declared: *'We are on the*

brink of victory. We have the Government troops out-gunned and surrounded in the capital, and throughout the rest of the country their power has disintegrated. The real battle is just about to start – that is the battle for a just and free Kaltrea.'

Since the monsoon began, the war has been going badly for the Government of President Sonchak. For the last year, there has been a steady flow of refugees attempting to cross the borders into neighbouring countries to escape the fighting. Their misery was compounded when the monsoons arrived unexpectedly early this year. Severe flooding cost the lives of an estimated ten thousand people, and many more have been made homeless. Up to a quarter of the country's population may now be threatened by disease and starvation as a result of the war and flood damage. The floods were also a major blow for the Government troops, as roads were made impassable and bridges swept away. The rebel forces, led by General Nyozhan, took advantage of the conditions to launch the counter-offensive that has brought them close to paralysing the country tonight. Informed sources believe that President Sonchak may flee the country within the next twenty-four hours if, as seems likely, the rebels gain control of the capital.

Foreign reaction to today's events has been quiet, with none of the major embassies in Amchuta releasing any statements. There is speculation that several multinational companies are set to withdraw from the country if the Government is toppled, as the PMRK is likely to nationalise the mining industry and restrict the export of capital as an early priority.

If the rebels do win the military battle against the Sonchak regime, it will be a personal triumph for 43 year old General Nyozhan, who has led the People's Movement for the Reconstruction of Kaltrea since its formation in 1983.

The PMRK began as a rallying ground for miners and steelworkers in the mineral rich northern province of Foonché. They complained of poor pay and dangerous working conditions, while the wealth from the mining industry was, they claimed, exported from the region to the fashionable south-west, where a system of Government incentives, both legal and corrupt, encouraged investment. The movement quickly grew into a national alliance of political groups and in the 1985 election, PMRK-supported candidates polled over one-third of the votes cast. However, supporters of the victorious Kaltrean National Congress of President Sonchak alleged widespread ballot rigging and intimidation of voters.

In a climate of increasing civil unrest, President Sonchak suspended Parliament early last year, and declared a state of emergency. The PMRK was banned from public organisation, following claims that they were responsible for several acts of terrorism and arson in the capital. The President appealed for national unity to prevent civil war, and accused the PMRK of being controlled by foreign governments. General Nyozhan's response was to go underground, using the well-established network of PMRK groups to build a guerrilla army that now looks unstoppable.

- Write up your new script, or if you have taken a photocopy, delete the rejected bits in red pen.

- What did you remove and why?
- How did you pinpoint the exact editing point?
- Compare your edited report with those of other individuals or groups. How does their emphasis differ from your own?
- How well does your report score on these points:
    - captures attention
    - represents all sides of the matter
    - makes clear the causes of the war and the issues at stake
    - allows the people involved to state their own case
    - says exactly what has happened today
    - says exactly what has led to today's events
    - points to future possibilities

The effects of editing are not obvious to viewers, who cannot guess what has been left out. Much editing is retrospective: it involves cutting away material which has been gathered. But there is another form of editing, which happens before pictures are taken. This is when stories are rejected as unimportant or uninteresting. They have, in effect, been edited out in the minds of the news team, so they never reach us. The qualities that make a potential story 'newsworthy' are not self-evident. They are determined by news values which have become so familiar that they go unnoticed.

News Appeal

Today, news can reach our homes within minutes. A plane crashes, and, within the hour, satellites and electronic communications have spread the news to millions of homes around the world. We can see pictures on our television sets tonight of a war being waged on another continent; we can watch an athlete re-enact a gold medal performance from this afternoon; we can go over live to the steps of Downing Street – but why?

Instant news

- Take a pen and spend a few minutes recalling the stories on last night's news. Number them in the order in which they appeared in the bulletin, and estimate the number of minutes spent on each story.
- How easy did you find this exercise? Retaining the news is more difficult than it seems. If your teacher has noted the bulletins, you can check your list and estimate how much you remembered.

News bulletins make us feel well informed, but, like entertainment programmes, their appeal is instant and soon fades. Some ten million people watch the news every day, putting it amongst the top ten programmes. The items are short, so our attention does not flag, and the issues are important. Bulletins have all the appeal of real-life drama. Indeed, many of them touch on our own lives, particularly when they concern government policy. So we watch and listen, and feel we are in the know – but the sensation is something of an illusion. We do not remember much of the news.

In fact, we don't have to remember the news, for bulletins occur throughout the day, updating and revising the stories.

- When is the best time of day to catch a news bulletin?
- Why do you think the stations time them this way?
- Do the different bulletins appeal to a different audience? Who might they be, and is the news 'angled' for them?

Like all programmes, the news has to win an audience. The pressure is on to provide stories which have the ring of urgency and significance. No matter how much or how little happens in a day, there are the same number of minutes in the bulletin. News has to be built up and made worthy of the time. Ironically, a good day for the news team is one full of conflict and disaster. There is a part of us all that relishes the most sensational stories, and the stations compete to deliver them the fastest.

- In groups, discuss the issues raised by the following news items. You have just one minute on each of them:

1 A top politician is in court today for divorce proceedings. Rumours are flying.

- Why should *you* hear the details of the case on the television news?

2 A train has crashed. There is devastation – wreckage – bodies. The news cameras were on the spot within minutes.

- What problems are raised by showing such pictures on the main news bulletins?

3 It is Budget day. Much of the news is spent listening in as the Chancellor makes his Budget speech. There are few surprises.

- What is the urgency? In what sense is this news?

4 There has been no change in the famine situation in a small country in Africa. Fifty people are dying every day at the emergency feeding camp. It's been the same for weeks now. The story has been reported several times.

- Is it news?
- What are the risks of repeating the report?
- What are the risks of not repeating the report?

Relative values

Source: Oxfam

Because there is this drive for fresh news, broadcasters favour items which are new, make good pictures and seem dramatic. But many important issues have none of these things. A long-standing famine in Africa may be more important than a recent political matter, but will it have 'news appeal'? And if the tragic pictures of starving children inspire the generosity of viewers, do they give a fair picture of the African people?

The victims of famine are sad spectacles on the television news. They appear to be passive. Not people who have jobs, political opinions, skills, and lives of their own. Unwittingly, the news makes them appear pathetic and helpless. It invites the well-fed Western viewer to look down on them as objects for pity.

- Think of the images of famine victims you have seen in television reports. Imagine yourself in their position as the camera approaches. What do you see when you look through their eyes? Picture the scene. How do you feel as the camera settles on you? How do you behave?

Relief groups working in famine-struck areas have become increasingly concerned about the images of starvation which we in the West accept. They have made a huge effort to provide more positive images of famine victims, because they have learnt that self-help is preferable to laid-on charity. These terrible images evoke compassion, but they also evoke condescension. People who give generously for emergency food may be less moved by appeals for ongoing assistance.

The crisis syndrome

There is a sort of crisis mentality in the news. It is always nice to know of a successful corn harvest, but we enjoy a good row more. A picket line makes better pictures than weeks of negotiation. An air crash is more dramatic than a safe day at Heathrow. The news favours stories of crises which are immediate and visual.

- Watch a news bulletin and note the nature of the stories. What is the ratio of 'good' news to 'bad' news?
- What 'good' news have you seen reported recently?
- Where in the news bulletin is the slot for 'good' news?

The overall impression is that important news is bad news. We often exclaim 'The news is awful tonight!' Anything that happens in the world seems to be disruptive. If only the trade unions would settle down, if only the money market were stable, if only the people of the Middle East would make friends . . . the whole world seems intent on 'rows', 'disputes', 'scandals' and 'rumpus'. Why can't these people in the news be more like us?

- Are there people in the news who *are* like you?
- What sort of stories do they appear in?

Bad news makes us hope for a world without conflict. It implies that there is a 'normal' world of calm and order, but disasters, terrorists, politicians keep it just beyond our grasp. Until we become involved in a conflict ourselves, we are inclined to feel one of the 'silent majority'. The unspoken message of the news is that normal people don't go on strike, don't hold controversial views, don't get over-involved, and don't have passionate commitments.

So it is with a shake of the head that we watch the latest crisis on the news bulletin. Some of the bigger stories linger in the memory.

- Do you remember these crises in the news? Who featured in them and what were they about? When did they happen?
    - The Westland Helicopter Affair
    - Spycatcher
    - The American Hostages
    - The Zeebrugge Ferry Disaster
    - Chernobyl

- What are the crises of today?

The catalogue of evils rolls by on the screen. Dissent, disorder and disaster seem to rule. Can this be the same world we live in – the world of family, school and friends? It is the same world, of course, and the news leaves us feeling glad to be in a safe corner of it. News always happens somewhere else to someone else.

In this way, the news insulates us. We feel safe in our private world, in our own living-room, with the television flickering reassuringly in the corner. The newscaster's face is friendly and familiar, the tone is calm and reasonable. Horrific as the news is, it is delivered to us from a distance. We are informed, but not involved. We can switch off quite unperturbed, both literally and mentally.

- Is it a good thing or a bad thing, to be protected in this way?

Working with rushes

This exercise relates to the Scottish Television videocassette containing the rushes of the Glasgow health workers' demonstration report featured in *A News Story in the Making*. Details of this cassette appear on page 5. The transcript of the final report can be found on pages 70–1.

'Rushes' is a term used to describe the original footage taken by the news camera team, and from which the report is compiled. The rushes in this case last 45 minutes, comprising a wide range of shots, interviews and speeches. Less than a tenth of this is used in the transmitted report.

At first glance, the pictures seem haphazard and disjointed. The camera zooms back and forth, frequently refocusing on different details. This is not due to clumsiness; the camera operator is picking out suitable shots in the knowledge that only brief clips will be used in the final report.

The figure in the top left corner of the screen is called the time code. You can use it to quickly locate any shot.

The rushes are taken back to the editing suite where the reporter and the editor select and organise the material and add a commentary. Time is short, and there is no written transcript. Decisions about what to include and how to phrase the commentary are made very quickly.

Study the rushes and consider the following questions:

1. Listen to the main speech of the demonstration made by Campbell Christie. Bearing in mind the pressures of time, which bit of his speech would you include to convey the gist of his argument?
   Compare this with the chosen extract which appeared in the final report (pages 70–1).

2. Study the various shots of the Glasgow demonstration – close ups of speakers, wide shots of demonstrators, banners, overhead panoramas, etc. Which shots best convey the size and nature of the rally?
   Compare these with the shots used in the final report.

3. Study the following interviews and speeches:
   - Campbell Christie's speech to the rally (04:50 to 09:50)
   - The interview with the Western Infirmary picket line (17:00 to 19:00)
   - The interview with Laurence Peterken (38:25 to 40:25)

   What differences do you notice in the conditions of interview? How do these conditions assist or hinder the speaker in representing his or her case to the viewer? How does the setting influence the viewer's reaction to the speaker?

4. The counter-demonstration receives only a few seconds in the final report. Is this short time justified?

5. The final report is limited to the available material contained in the rushes. It therefore follows that the members of the news team must decide in advance what they want to include in the report. Do you think there are any important areas ignored in the rushes, i.e. which were never intended for inclusion?

6. Having seen the rushes, would you say that the final report offers a fair overview of the day's events? What news angle does it adopt to present the story? Do you think there is an alternative angle which could have been taken, using the same resources?

Special Project: Local News Bulletin

The object of the exercise

The object of this day-long practical activity is to produce a live local news bulletin lasting about 10 minutes to show to a selected audience.

Aims

1 To gain an inside understanding of the practical and political considerations which shape the news.

2 To gain confidence from experience in:
- operating video equipment
- co-operating in teamwork
- taking responsibility and making decisions
- dealing with people outside
- working under pressure
- putting your work on the line

Advance preparations

1 Decide who is to be *the audience*. If you are based in a school or college, you might choose to show it to another class, an assembly or a parents' evening. Issue an invitation if necessary.

2 Choose a convenient *date* for making the bulletin. Have a fall-back date in case of rain.

3 Fix the broadcast *time*. Showing the bulletin 30 minutes before the end of the working day will leave time for some over-running and an orderly dismissal.

4 Find out what video *equipment* is available and book it, along with extra rooms and materials as necessary.

5 Decide on the *area to be covered* by the bulletin, so that people can watch out for relevant news stories.

6 Allocate *jobs*. The list on page 83 can be adjusted to suit your requirements. You may have to double up on jobs, or expand the number of news teams, depending on the size of your group.

7 Get into reporting groups to *review the likely stories*. Keep an eye on the development of national news stories which may have a local angle, as well as stories running in the local newspapers. You may have heard of potential stories yourself. Don't neglect this 'on site' knowledge.

8 Obtain any *permissions* in advance, for example to record particular interviews and events.

What you will need

A set of morning papers
The most recent local newspapers
Local map
As many local information booklets as possible
Video equipment
Pens, paper, clipboards

FACING THE FACTS

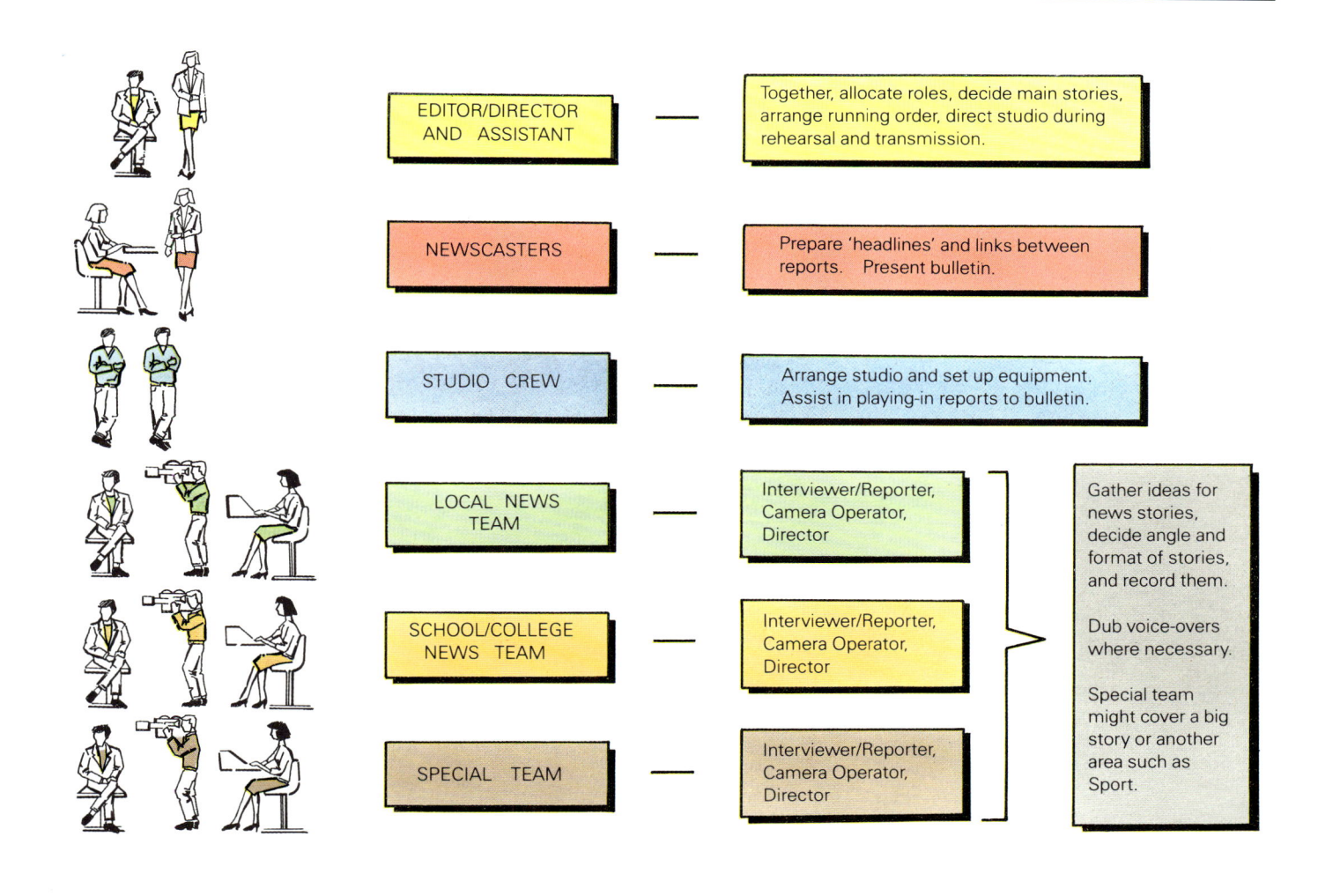

EDITOR/DIRECTOR AND ASSISTANT	Together, allocate roles, decide main stories, arrange running order, direct studio during rehearsal and transmission.
NEWSCASTERS	Prepare 'headlines' and links between reports. Present bulletin.
STUDIO CREW	Arrange studio and set up equipment. Assist in playing-in reports to bulletin.
LOCAL NEWS TEAM	Interviewer/Reporter, Camera Operator, Director
SCHOOL/COLLEGE NEWS TEAM	Interviewer/Reporter, Camera Operator, Director
SPECIAL TEAM	Interviewer/Reporter, Camera Operator, Director

Gather ideas for news stories, decide angle and format of stories, and record them.

Dub voice-overs where necessary.

Special team might cover a big story or another area such as Sport.

Ways of adapting numbers

This arrangement is based on a group of 15 people. You will have to adjust the numbers to fit your group. You could drop the special team, or reduce the team numbers, but it is better if people double up on jobs, joining a news team in the morning and filling one of the other roles during rehearsal and transmission.

On the day

1 *Finalise* your choice of stories for the bulletin.
2 Draw up a draft *running order* for the bulletin, showing the approximate length of each story.
3 The *timetable* of the day's activities shown on page 84 can be adapted to your requirements.
4 *Prepare a signing-out list*, so that your teacher will know who is where at any particular moment. Always sign out before you leave the classroom.
5 *Advice* about the recording techniques can be found in the section entitled *Try It Yourself* on page 128.

	EDITOR DIRECTOR ASSISTANT	**NEWSCASTERS**	**CAMERA OPERATOR**	**NEWS TEAMS**
FIRST THING	Re-allocate roles of absentees. Put up a 'signing-out' sheet. Help gather ideas for news stories.	Collect newspapers and research material. Help gather ideas for news stories.	Collect and check equipment. Help gather ideas for news stories.	Gather ideas for news stories – scour newspapers – ask around – local radio news.
MORNING	Gather ideas together and decide on main stories. Join a news team. Review material brought in by news teams. Find out afternoon plans.	Join a news team. Review material brought in by news teams.	Join a news team.	Prepare list of possible stories for editor. Research stories and go out to record them. Remember to prepare interview questions, reports etc in advance. Bring back material to show to editor and newscasters.
LUNCHTIME				
AFTERNOON	Brief the group on progress so far. Announce a provisional running-order. Suggest convenient lengths for afternoon stories.	Prepare news 'headlines' to open the bulletin. Write links and introductions. Note down 'cues' for video reports.	Set up camera + monitor. Arrange studio set. Learn 'cues'.	Afternoon stories to collect. Dub voice-overs where necessary.
MID-AFTERNOON	Review afternoon stories. Finalise schedule. Post up running order with times.	Rehearsal.	Rehearsal.	Deadline. All material to the editor. Set up viewing room. Rehearsal: comments? Organise audience.
REHEARSAL	Rehearsal: responsible for timing and loading playing-in video reports			
	Bulletin.	Bulletin.	Bulletin.	
AFTERWARDS		Return materials.	Return equipment.	Clear up and rearrange furniture.

FACING THE FACTS

Setting up the equipment

There are several ways of transmitting the bulletin, depending on the equipment available. Consult your teacher or the person responsible for audio-visual equipment about the best arrangement. If you can introduce your recorded reports into the 'live' bulletin, the best layout uses two rooms:

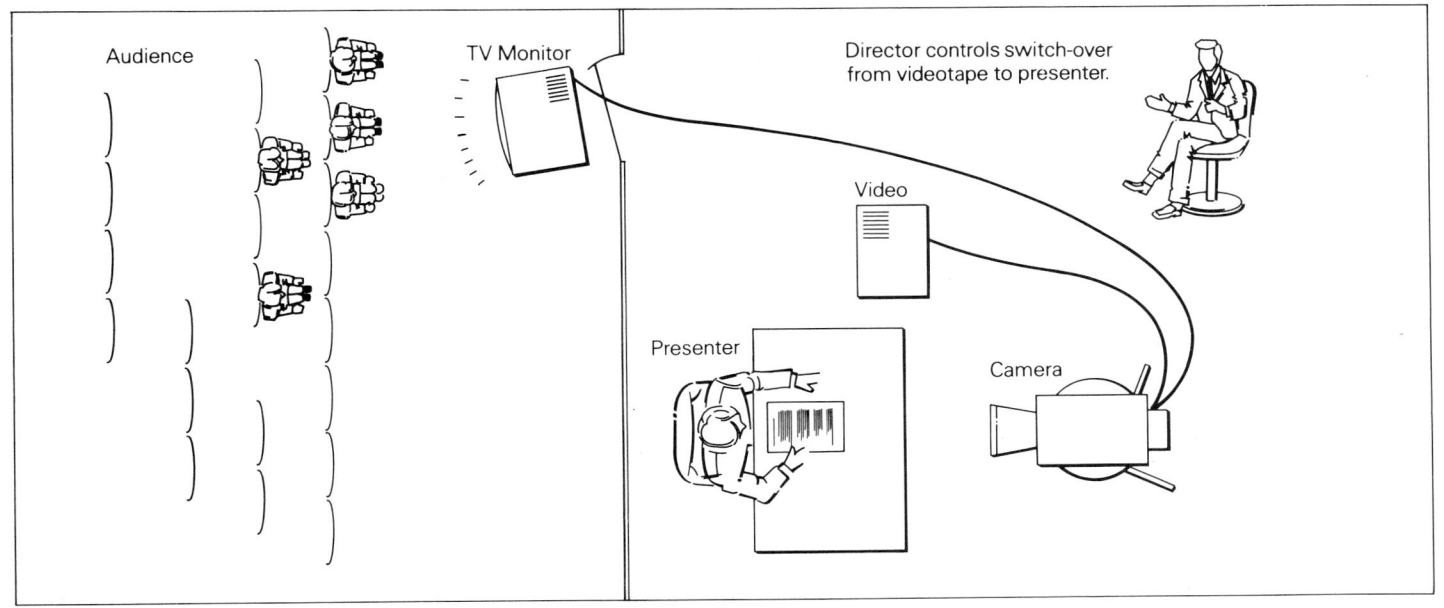

The setting up can be tricky, so rehearse the switch from camera to tape several times. The director should note the last few seconds of each recorded item so that the newscaster can be given a 'cue' to start the next link.

If your equipment cannot cut between recorded and live material, the newscaster can address the audience directly, pausing for the recorded reports:

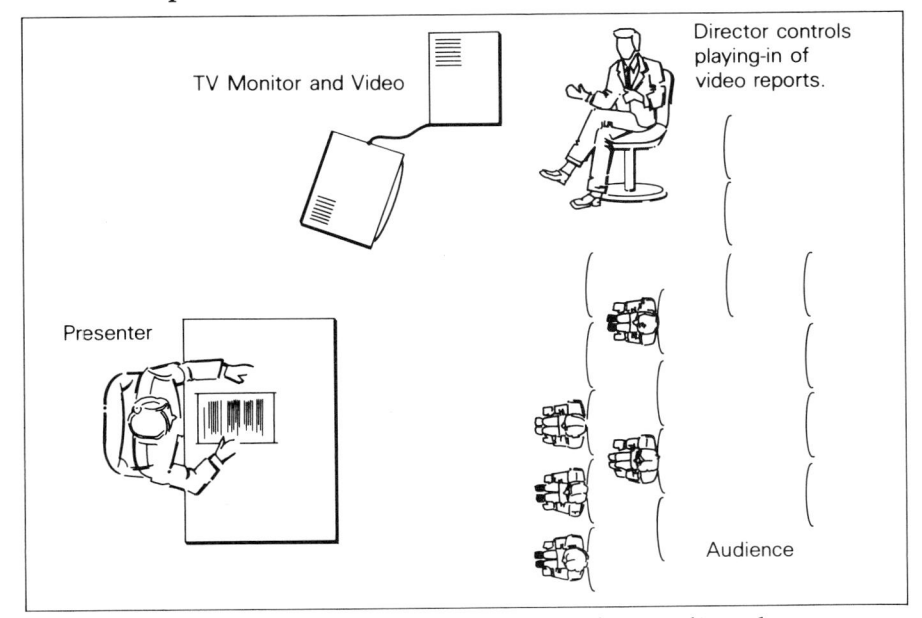

Discuss with your teacher the possibility of recording the newscasters at work, so that they can see their own performances later on.

For homework

Write an account of your activities during the day, paying attention to the following points:

- What did you find interesting, surprising and frustrating about the experience?
- Which parts of the video were the most successful – and why?
- Review your own attitude towards the exercise and what you may have learnt from it.
- On reflection, what might you do differently another time?

Next lesson

In groups, watch the recorded material and share the comments you prepared for homework. Discuss the following points:

- What were the most successful elements of the bulletin?
- What were the major constraints in making the news bulletin?
- What considerations determined the treatment or angle of the stories?
- What considerations determined the length and order of the items?
- How far did the medium itself – the camerawork, performance, technical equipment – enable or obstruct the reporting of news?

PART THREE
The Art of Persuasion

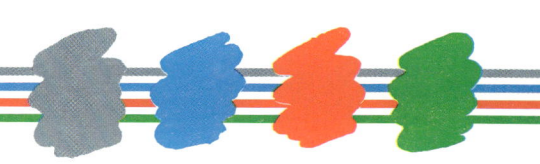

Making a Television Advertisement

Television advertisements are produced by teams of designers, actors and writers who work to tight specifications. The product, the intended audience and the purpose – to create customers – are all pinpointed in advance. The impact of the advertisement must be instant and attractive, packing information and appeal into a few seconds. When the Trustee Savings Bank launched their new 'Foundation Homeplan' mortgage package, they turned to an advertising agency to come up with ideas for a television campaign to reach potential customers.

The work begins with writers and artists putting their heads together to produce an outline for the advertisement. But there are tight constraints. First, there is limited time – in this case just 40 seconds – to put over some basic information and to impress likely customers. There is also a particular audience to be appealed to – mostly couples buying their first home. The designers seek a selling angle – will it be funny? – will it debunk the competition? – will it tell a story?

At first it does: the designers come up with a modern-day fairy tale in which our hero and our heroine go in search of a mortgage like sheep amongst wolves. They are hounded by conmen, slick talkers, and doorstep heavies, all giving conflicting advice, until at last they enter into the sane, straight-talking world of the TSB.

The advertising agency presents the proposal to the TSB for their reactions. The TSB would prefer to emphasise the bank as the first port of call, rather than the last. They want to identify the TSB as friendly, approachable and sympathetic.

THE ART OF PERSUASION

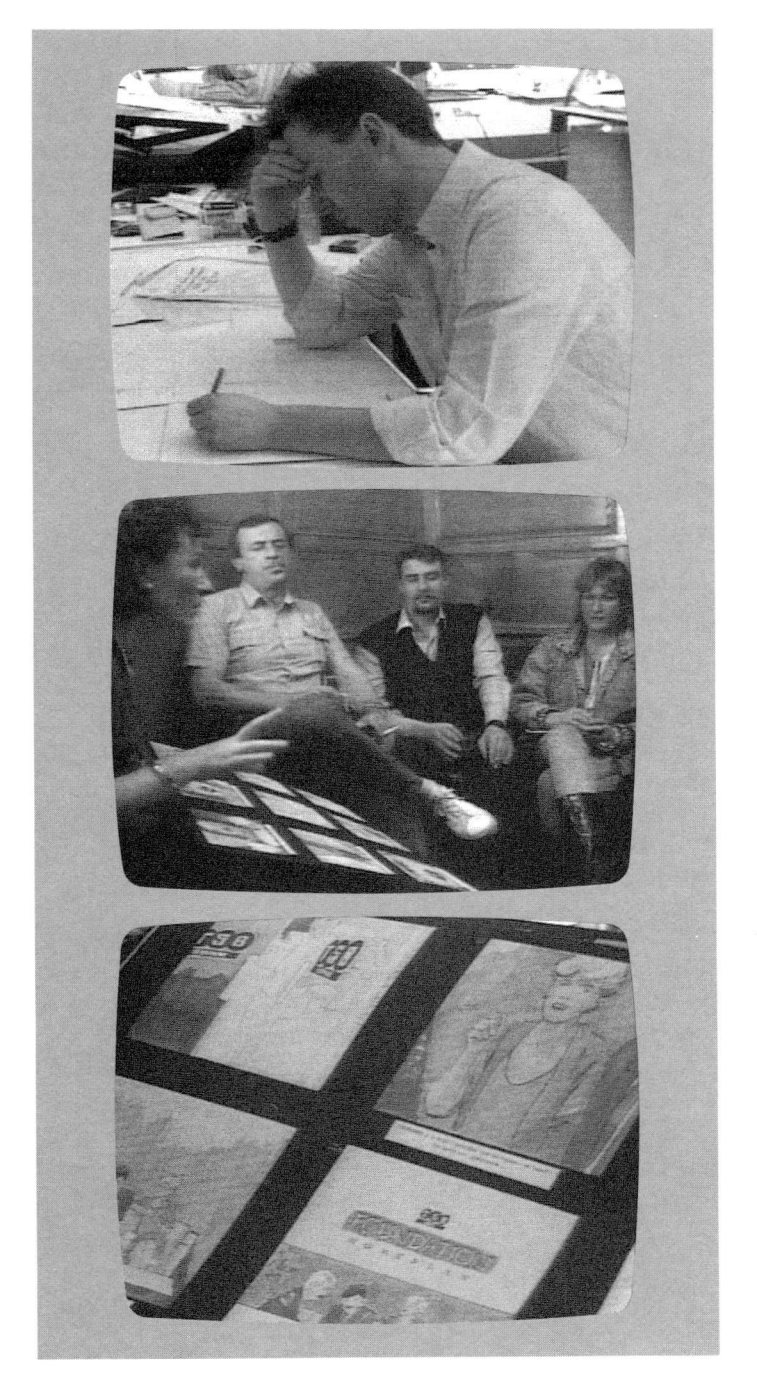

Back at the drawing board, the designers think again, retaining the strong parts of the original idea and reworking them into a new format. The result is drawn up into a sequence of coloured sketches – a storyboard – with dialogue, and the new proposal is considered again by the TSB. They are satisfied with the new approach.

Some likely customers – members of the target audience – are invited to share their responses to the advertisement. Researchers show them the storyboard, and question them about its appeal. The results are good. Those on the panel feel the advertisement offers a positive image of the bank, and they identify with the couple when they are besieged by the fast-talking salesmen of the opposition.

The problems are not over. The IBA (Independent Broadcasting Authority) looks over all advertisements to see that they keep to guidelines concerning what is proper and acceptable in the battle for customers. Nowhere is competition fiercer than in the world of banking, and the IBA is not happy with the portrayal of the opposition in the proposal. The agency redesigns the advertisement to meet the IBA's requirements, and the team moves on to the next stage of production.

The script/storyboard is developed for the screen by the director, whose professional expertise lies in directing the cameras and the actors. Unless he has the right material recorded now, it will be too late to amend it at a later stage. In his mind, he has to hold a picture of the finished product: a strong, attention-grabbing opening, a high-powered piece of acting from an over-eager salesman, a long reassuring shot as the camera eye enters the bank. Ideas continue to develop as they go through the stages of practical production.

While the advertisement is edited, dubbed and tailored to the 40 seconds available, the media director is deciding the best time and channel on which to screen it. She relies on figures from BARB – the Broadcasters Audience Research Board. These are weekly statistics showing who is watching which programmes. The figures include breakdowns of the number, location, social class and age of the viewers. Although the peak time audience is huge, it is very expensive to show an advertisement then, and there may be cheaper times of the day when first-time buyers are likely to be watching.

The success of an advertisement is judged by the sales it generates. Since showing, hundreds of people on the verge of house-buying have been prompted to go along to the TSB. Attracting their custom has been the chief consideration all along: every decision in the production process has been made with that in mind.

Making a Market

Constructing advertisements

Advertisements evolve in a different way from the programmes made by broadcast television. In the first place, they are commissioned by companies with the explicit purpose of selling their products. The advertising agencies organise the creation, production and distribution of the advertisement.

The purpose, audience and specifications of the advertisement are highly defined. The chain of command starts with the client – a company, perhaps, which has something to sell:

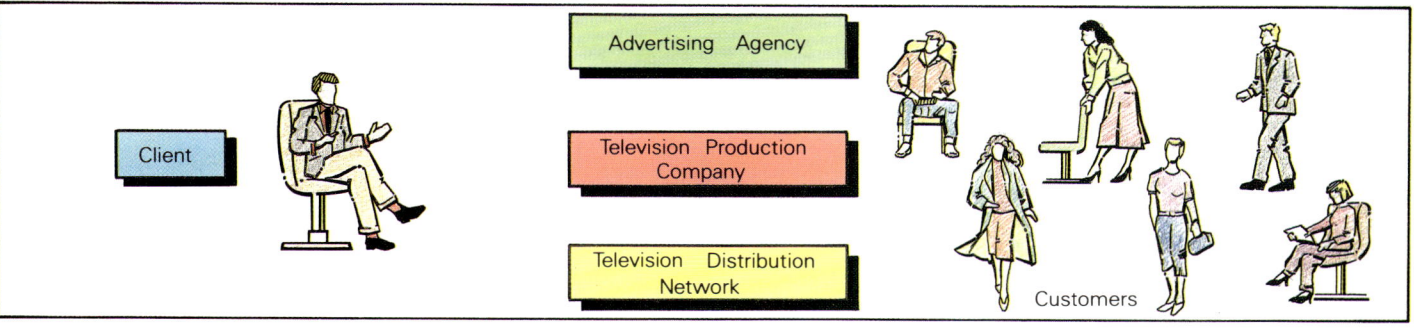

The advertising agency thinks up an idea for the advertisement and presents it in storyboard form for the comments of the client, potential customers and controlling bodies such as the IBA. After satisfying these different groups, the agency employs a television production company to shoot the advertisement.

Great attention is paid to details. Advertisers are prepared to invest heavily in time and resources to ensure the best possible effect, and the budget for such productions is very high compared with that for most programmes. Each shot is thought through in scrupulous detail. In the TSB advertisement already mentioned, the director decided to recreate the bank scene from the point of view of a customer entering the bank, by using one long shot from the door to a couple discussing their mortgage. He explains to the client and to the advertising agency how it will work:

> In the second half there could be a danger of the commercial actually coming to a standstill, right? So the whole point about trying to achieve this sequence all in one shot and getting that effect of someone walking in and the camera actually going through the door and sweeping round, taking in the whole of the bank – and we're using one of the existing branches now – and then we're straight into this settee situation – it will visually give you the ability to keep the rhythm going but it will become kind of smooth, which will add to the effect that you're trying to create there.
>
> **Director, TSB advertisement**

The director's main concern is that the advertisement is practical to shoot and appealing to the viewer. His first task is to bring a practical eye to the storyboard. His role is central as the actors are assembled and shooting begins. Action is rehearsed over and over again until it is perfect. Here the director gives instructions to the two actors who open the advertisement:

> This is the front end of the commercial, right? I would like you to start sitting down and start talking once you've started to move down, right? A general note to both the artists: let's get the pace really moving on this one...
>
> **Director, TSB advertisement**

Notice how conscious the director must be of the advertisement's format: short, punchy and pacy. Every consideration is geared to the demands of time and direct customer appeal.

This attention to detail and concentrated messages is also apparent in other elements of the production. Even the colour of the set is closely scrutinised:

> The other thing I looked at was primary colours... so this is good. So we're going to keep it quite monochromatic, take out all the artificial plants which are just ghastly, put in some, you know, a couple of nice big trees. All the clothes that I thought that the people in the end-thing would be wearing would be kind of mid-tone, not anything too dark, not anything too light, just creams or pinks...
>
> **Set designer, TSB advertisement**

- In groups, discuss the differences between advertisements and programmes such as those considered in 'Just Like Life?' Consider the following areas:

    – finance
    – format
    – purpose
    – lifespan
    – how ideas start and evolve

Each advertisement starts from a product to be marketed: a consumer item such as a jar of coffee, a service such as an airline or something as general as a large corporation producing many products – such as ICI, BP or Allied Lyons. In themselves, many of these products are rather dull and there may be little to distinguish them from their competitors, so the job of the agency is to give each one a special appeal. A humorous advertisement, for example, may help to give the product an upbeat and friendly image.

- Consider a number of advertisements and discuss what strategy the advertiser uses to give the product a positive and appealing image.
- Watch an advertisement for a bank and consider how you would react if you represented a competing bank. What kind of campaign would you launch to win over the customers who might otherwise be wooed by the opposition?

Audience targeting

Television advertisements cost many thousands of pounds for each screening. At peak times, such as the early evening, television can promise audiences of over 10 million. For some advertisers, this is an expensive but guaranteed time to reach potential customers. For others, it's not so good. What if the people watching are not the people who would buy their product? It's no use advertising business computers when the executives are at work, or advertising toys when the kids have gone to bed. In these cases, it makes more sense to search for a time when the right audience, though smaller, will be watching.

- Think about it. Who will be watching at these times on a *weekday*?

    6.45 am
    9.00 am
    11.30 am
    4.45 pm
    6.00 pm

    7.30 pm
    9.30 pm
    11.30 pm

- What differences might there be in the audience watching at:

    10.30 am weekday
    10.30 am Saturday
    10.30 am Sunday

    3.00 pm weekday
    3.00 pm Saturday
    3.00 pm Sunday

- How might the audience differ in size, needs, and spending power, at the following times of the year:

    – early January
    – early August

    – early November
    – just before Christmas

- It is late Autumn. You are an advertiser. What time of day and week would you choose to place an advertisement for the following:

    – instant coffee
    – a personal computer
    – lager
    – toys
    – British Petroleum
    – a holiday company

    – British Telecom
    – a bank
    – instant meals
    – an employment agency for temporary office staff

Consumers

- Who buys products? Think carefully about this. The person who pays for the product is not necessarily the person who selects and uses it. Who would you most expect to choose the product in these cases:

    - clothes for a new-born baby
    - clothes for a toddler
    - toys for a 5 year old
    - shoes for an 11 year old
    - school equipment (for example, maths equipment)
    - a bouquet
    - clothes for the older man
    - a second car
    - jewellery
    - the weekly shop

- How might this sort of information affect the time of screening and the advertising approach?

Sometimes the target audience is easy to identify – but when do those customers watch television? For example, what assumptions can you make about the viewing habits of potential customers for:

- low alcohol lager
- a large hatchback car
- slimming aids
- expensive garden furniture

- When would be the best time of year to mount a campaign for each of these products and when would be the best time of day to transmit the advertisement?

Businesses are always on the look-out for new audiences and new products. They are searching for opportunities to cash in on a popular need. In other words, they create a market which did not exist before. What opportunities might an advertiser see in these people:

- someone who has just turned 18
- someone who has just retired
- a first-time parent
- someone who has just become a student
- someone setting up home for the first time

- What kind of products might these people consider which they hadn't previously noticed?
- What problems may face an advertiser in getting such people to recognise their need for the product?

Study the transcript of an advertisement opposite and discuss the questions below:

THE ART OF PERSUASION

The advertisement opens with a long shot of two men strolling through an orchard.

ELDER MAN: Let's walk. I'm adding your proposals to tomorrow's agenda.
YOUNG MAN: Yes, but will you back them?
ELDER MAN: Say I was a Midland customer – and buying a new home's no picnic – what are you going to do for me?
YOUNG MAN: We'd start by offering you the right kind of mortgage.
ELDER MAN: Well, doesn't everybody?
YOUNG MAN: Not with a half per cent off the interest rate for a year!
ELDER MAN: Ah, money, huh? Suppose I say there's more to it than that – there are things like security, the future . . .

A shot of children filling an apple basket.

YOUNG MAN: As a bank, we offer you financial counselling – confidential advice on how to manage your money.
ELDER MAN: What if I'm not with the Midland?
YOUNG MAN: You don't have to be – you still benefit.

They pass a branch laden with fruit.

ELDER MAN: And later on . . . when the family starts to grow? Will you still be listening then?
YOUNG MAN: Yes, enough to make it easier to use your house as security . . . free the money you've invested in it, for the family, say, or for something unforeseen. Who knows what might happen tomorrow?

They cross a picturesque bridge over a stream.

ELDER MAN: Oh I think tomorrow's going to turn out fine, just fine.
VOICE-OVER: ORCHARD . . . THE LIVING MORTGAGE FROM THE LISTENING BANK.

- What is the advertisement selling?
- Who is the target audience?
- How is its appeal strengthened by

    – the relationship between the two men
    – the setting
    – the references to tomorrow's meeting

- What is there in the advertisement to attract the trust of new customers?

Advertisers used to use social class as a way of analysing audiences. They aimed their products at particular income groups. They have now discovered it is more effective to group people broadly according to their self image, because this affects the kind of lifestyle they admire.

There are four main categories: the *succeeders* – people who see themselves as powerful, effective and successful; the *aspirers* who see themselves reaching up for promotion, progress and a better lifestyle; the *carers* who see themselves as socially responsible and caring, with humane values; and the *mainstreamers*, who see themselves as established, safe and comfortably off. It is important to realise that these categories describe the way people see themselves – not necessarily how they really are. And many people do not fit neatly into these categories: there is a growing trend in advertisements which appeal to *individualists*, people who see themselves as lone spirits.

Look over a handful of advertisements from peak viewing time – the early evening – and work out which market each one aims at.

Product identity

Advertisers are quick to use the strengths of television to fix an image of the product in the viewer's mind. Familiar graphics, catchy jingles and memorable phrases all bombard the memory. Can you identify the products which go with these 'identities':

Graphic identities

Verbal identities
- At the sign of the black horse – a thoroughbred among banks
- The listening bank
- Probably the best lager in the world
- It's good but not that good
- When a man you don't know buys you flowers . . .
- That will do nicely
- Vorsprung Durch Technik

Musical identities
Hum the music which you associate with the following products:
- Martini
- Old Spice
- Levi's
- Harp
- Just Juice
- Fairy Liquid

Name identities

Even the names of products make use of the suggestive quality of words. What is suggested by the names of the following perfumes:

- Rive Gauche
- Le Jardin
- Impulse
- Charlie

What trends can you identify in the names of:

- models of cars
- lagers
- perfume for men
- shampoo

Campaign strategy

Advertisers use all the art of language to sell their products. The language of the advertisement 'packages' the product just as much as the wrapper it comes in. Many advertisements tell us explicitly that the product is bigger, better, faster, longer-lasting, cleaner, safer, surer than any other. Think of products currently advertised on television which claim to be:

- new improved versions of themselves
- free from any added ingredients
- enhanced with a special added ingredient
- pure

- What other familiar selling points can you think of?

One of the greatest problems facing advertisers is competition when there is little to choose between the various products on the market. Advertisers often resort to subtle attacks on their competitors. List all the advertisements you have seen on television for:

- lager
- credit cards
- rail and air transport
- banks and building societies
- cat food
- toothpaste
- washing powder

- Pick out the ones which either directly or indirectly refer to the competition.
- What does the product claim to do better than its competitors?
- How is the competition put in its place?

Devise a campaign strategy for a series of television advertisements featuring the products described overleaf.

1 Half-calorie chocolates in a gift box.

2 A diet pack, containing a week's supply of calorie counted bars, soups and biscuits.

3 A range of disposable underwear.

4 Expensive clothes for the under-eights with a continental designer label.

5 A national daily doorstep delivery service of milk, newspapers, packed lunches, breakfast food, TV and radio details and other 'daily' products.

6 A campaign to persuade people to cut down on salt, which causes adverse effects on blood pressure, arteries and the heart.

- For each product, identify:
    - the target audience
    - the lifestyle they would most like to have
    - the competition
    - the best time to show the advertisements

- For each product, create:
    - a product name
    - a by-line or catchphrase
    - a cartoon storyboard outlining the idea for a television advertisement (see p. 129)

- How far does the information in the first exercise — identifying audience, aspirations, competition and timing — influence the design of the campaign itself?

Creating Consumers

Positioning the viewer

Advertisements address an imaginary consumer: you. You are invited to take part in the advertisement by working out its meaning and acting on it. And the message is always the same: buy me.

In effect, an advertisement asks you to collaborate with it so that you end up identifying with the product it represents. It draws you in to feel part of its world.

As soon as you look at a television picture, you adopt the position of the camera. You see events from its point of view. If the camera looks up, so do you; if the camera rises above it all, so do you. Already the advertisement has you 'placed' where it wants you.

The advertisement below, for example, was part of a magazine advertising campaign. Study its details with care.

When the occasion arises, only one sherry rises to it.

HARVEYS BRISTOL CREAM. THE BEST SHERRY IN THE WORLD

- Where do you seem to watch from?
- Which of the people are you most invited to identify with?
- How do you come to identify with them?
- Imagine the scene just a second or two later. What will have changed?
- Why has the advertiser chosen this exact moment to sell the product?
- How does the advertisement secure your sympathy, trust and attention?
- The advertisement does not make a direct appeal to the audience to buy the sherry. So how does it encourage people to do so?

Many advertisements make an indirect appeal to the consumer, inviting them to share a joke, or work out a puzzle. There are, in fact, some bizarre advertisements which attract attention simply because they are so difficult to understand. It is a clever way to get consumers to concentrate on the pictures, and to fix the product name in the mind.

- Can you think of any advertisements which are deliberately bizarre or puzzling?
- How do they work?

Needs and promises

We all have needs which extend beyond immediate survival. As human beings, we are hungry for new experiences. Advertisers know this and suggest to us that their products can fulfil our wider needs. They often can. But there are no guarantees, though advertisements imply there are. They make promises we want to believe.

Most of all, they offer us lifestyles we want to have. A convenience food sells itself as a useful idea for people whose lives are busy with sport, social engagements and business meetings. Buying the product is a way of identifying with such a lifestyle without the demands of actually living it. We buy more than the product – we buy an image.

The world we see in the background of an advertisement is carefully designed, because it is part of the product image. Think of an example of each of the following:

Advertisements which feature places such as:

- an exotic location
- a fabulous home
- a romantic setting
- a comic 'stage set' world

Advertisements which feature people who are:

- executive business types
- beautiful and self-possessed women
- incredibly sophisticated and cool
- confident and articulate
- highly individual and nonconformist

Advertisements in which people enjoy:

- a wonderful social life
- a successful career
- a close and loving family
- a healthy, outgoing lifestyle
- a life full of surprises and change
- sex appeal

- How relevant are these images to the product?
- In what way do advertisers imply that the product can secure these lifestyles for the consumer?

There are some advertisements which push aside these attractive but unlikely people in favour of characters who are 'just like ordinary people'. Many of these advertisements are directed at mums in the traditional family set-up. They feature a 'typical' housewife doing her shopping or going about her housework. Perhaps she is stopped by an interviewer to taste a new spread, or say which is the whiter of two washed shirts. Perhaps she is particularly pleased with her latest furniture polish or cook-in sauce.

- What kind of person is the 'typical housewife' of advertisements?
- What are her main interests in life?
- What is her husband like?
- What sort of house does she live in?
- Describe her children.

On the face of it, these 'ordinary' characters are more like us than the flamboyant types considered earlier. But in fact, only five per cent of families fit the traditional image – Dad working, Mum at home, two kids at school. The television family is just another fiction – an alternative way to win our trust and custom.

The world according to advertisements

Advertisements flatter consumers by implying they are people of discrimination and good sense. If the advertisement is cryptic, it flatters your insight. If it is funny, it flatters your sense of humour. It makes an insider of you by seeming to share a confidence. And people want to believe in the promises of advertisements.

Read through these outlines of television advertisements, and answer the questions that follow:

Slimming aids
She, slim as a whippet, long blonde hair and huge dewy eyes, nibbles with satisfaction at her low-calorie ration bar for today. A wonderfully arranged salad lies on her plate. A moment later, light as a fairy, she steps onto her scales, and draws a measuring tape around her waist. She is miraculously thin.

- Rewrite this scenario featuring someone who really needs to slim, with all the problems that poses.

Floor cleaner
Her kitchen is aflood with the soapy suds of her present floor cleaner. Those stubborn household stains just won't clean away. The baby is whining in its highchair, the dog is scratching at the door. Poor housewife! Enter the breezy neighbour – a trim, sensible woman who recommends New Floorshine. What a pal! Within seconds, they are finishing the floor, which gleams hygienically. The baby is smiling in its mother's arms and the dog sits quietly wagging its tail.

- Describe the scene four hours later.

Cocktail
A slick nightclub, very sophisticated. A couple, very cool. First date.
HIM: And for you?...
HER: I'd like a Coco-rumba... if you dare.
(*His eyes widen*)
HIM: (*suggestively*) Who dares... wins?
HER: I'll answer that... after my Coco-rumba.

> HIM: Make that two Coco-rumbas.
> (*Their lips tremble on their glasses*)
> COCO-RUMBA... IF YOU DARE.

- What would you be thinking in his/her shoes?

High Power Shower
The man in the shower is enjoying an invigorating shower. He soaps his hairy chest, shakes his hair and luxuriates in the pulsing steaming spray.

- You buy the high power shower. Next morning, bleary-eyed, you switch it on. How does it really feel?

Advertisements create an unreal world of perfection in which the product satisfies every desire. Nobody is fat in advertisements, not even the people who are slimming. It's hard to see why they need the low-calorie sweetener or revolutionary diet. Advertisements show the world as we would like it to be, where everyone is slim, healthy and content. In this paradise, no one need feel depressed, bored or apathetic. Another refreshing drink, a change of designer clothes, or an even faster car will soon put them right.

But the best of new cars breaks down, the baby spills its food on that dazzling, newly-cleaned floor, and the dinner still burns if it is left too long in the latest fan-assisted oven. Advertisements seem to promise an end to all that. As they finish, the dishes are always clean and the washing is as white as snow. But we have to live with our past, present, and future, while the people in the advertisements are happily marooned in a permanent 'now'. They have hardly tasted success before their part is over: the picture cuts to black and we are on to the next advertisement or programme.

The consumer trap

In the world of advertisements, everything is possible. It is a world filled with images of happiness, success, and satisfaction. And the advertisements suggest that we can share in this world by owning the products featured in it.

There is nothing wrong in wanting a better world for ourselves, and there are many products which do make life easier and more enjoyable. But the glamorous world of advertisements can make us feel that our own lives are humdrum and colourless. In whetting our appetite for better things, it casts a shadow over ordinary life. If we don't have the money to buy the product, it makes for frustration. If we do, we may well be disappointed, for no product can give total and everlasting satisfaction. And then we are caught in the consumer trap – as each new promise fails to satisfy, we chase the next, seeking but never achieving fulfilment.

- Name your three favourite advertisements.
- What is it about them which appeals to you?
- What secret promises do the advertisements make, to which you respond?

Talking Pictures

We are familiar with the rules of written and spoken language. We can change the way we present an issue by the words we choose. It is perhaps more difficult to consider pictures in the same way. But television is full of pictures, which have a subtle and persuasive language of their own. When a director plans the shot, he or she chooses the angle, position and distance of the camera to convey meaning in much the same way as the writer chooses words. Television advertisements often use the power of pictures to good effect, to describe and suggest the merits of the product in a very short time.

Setting

Where words would say, 'a car frees you to travel where you please', a picture shows it racing through the mountains of Europe. The result is an image of holiday adventure. We could, of course, be shown the car sitting in a traffic jam down the local High Street, but that wouldn't impress us half as much.

Consider the settings used in advertisements for these products:

- holidays
- cars
- computers
- spirits (such as white rum)
- employment agencies (such as those recruiting office staff)

- Do you detect any trends in the settings?
- How do you account for them?

Camera position

The angle of the camera obliges the viewer to see events in a particular way. For example, if the camera is placed to look upwards to a character, then we are made to look up to them too, and not just physically. We 'look up' to them as superiors. If the camera looks down on a character, then *we* feel superior. If we look a character in the eye, it is as though we are face to face as equals.

- Watch a television advertisement featuring children's goods (a weekday morning is a good time).
- Does the camera place you where the adults would be, or down with the children?
- Can you explain why?

It is not only the angle of the camera, but also its distance which is important. We become more intimate and observant close up. We can see facial details and expressions which aren't visible from a distance. We pay greater attention to the individual because we are not distracted by the surroundings. As we notice the emotions and reactions written on their faces, we become emotionally as well as physically closer.

So the camera compels us to share its view of events. This has important implications for factual programmes as well as drama.

- Over the next week, watch a few minutes of these television programmes:
    - a pop music show
    - a newscaster presenting a bulletin
    - a Sunday hymn service
- What do you notice about the distance of the camera from the subject in each case?
- What does the camera distance suggest about our relationship to the people?
- Which distance is most respectful?
- What implications does this have for news reporting?

Telling details

Like words, pictures can emphasise some points and not others. Many advertisements dwell in close-up detail on women's bodies – often the most erotic and vulnerable parts – eyes, lips, breasts, legs. The camera encourages the viewer to take in the sight of the woman, and makes of her a showpiece. This is what is meant when advertisers are accused of making women into sex objects. The camera assumes the right to come up close to the woman's body in a way it would never approach a newscaster, for example. There, the camera keeps a respectful distance. An advertisement for a cooking product may select quite different details of the woman. Her lips and buttocks are abandoned in favour of her competent hands and good-humoured face. Her jewellery receives less attention than her wedding ring. The emphasis is on woman as wife, housekeeper, and mother.

- Look at a variety of advertisements and pay attention to the way the camera treats the characters – the angle and distance.
- What details about the people are emphasised?
- What is the overall effect on our interpretation of the character?
- What differences do you notice in the treatment of men and women in advertisements?

Lighting

Lighting is a very suggestive element in any setting. Where soft, low lights may be romantic, brilliant primary colours can suggest fun and heat. Consider the lighting and colours used in the pictures on the next page.

- What mood is suggested by the lighting and colour used in each picture?

Lighting people's faces is particularly important in television because its strength lies in close-ups. Try this exercise in a darkened room. You will need a torch. Light a partner's face in different ways such as:

- upwards from under the chin
- sideways from a distance
- downwards from a foot or so, overhead
- face forwards

- What effects were created by the lighting?

The principal lamp used to light a character is called a *keylight*. Television studios usually use at least one other lamp as well – the *infill* light. This softens the shadows created by the keylight.

- Look at a few minutes of television and observe the lighting used on the faces of news presenters and characters in various dramas. Work out where the keylight is positioned and what effect the lighting has.
- Discuss the lighting and colour requirements for the following television scenes:

    - a close up of a vampire, just risen
    - a close up of a shy, gentle face
    - a suspect just surprised by the Secret Police
    - a prisoner in a bleak interrogation room
    - a sleazy night club
    - a romantic scene on a rug in front of a log fire

106 CONSTRUCTING TELEVISION

The Language of Persuasion

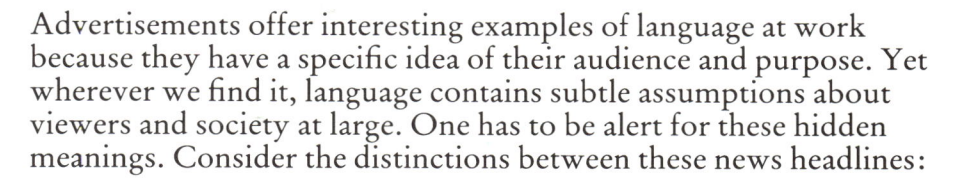

Advertisements offer interesting examples of language at work because they have a specific idea of their audience and purpose. Yet wherever we find it, language contains subtle assumptions about viewers and society at large. One has to be alert for these hidden meanings. Consider the distinctions between these news headlines:

Almost a hundred gathered to greet the Soviet premier.

Fewer than a hundred turned out to see the Russian arrive.

The details have to be finalised within 24 hours if the treaty is to be signed at this historic summit.

The treaty is held up by wrangling over minor points. Unless they are resolved before tomorrow, the leaders will go home empty-handed.

None of these statements lies, but language inevitably gives a particular angle on the things it describes. It interprets at the same time as telling.

Deciding how to say things on television is determined by many factors such as the supposed audience, the purpose of the broadcast, notions of what is proper, the type of presenter, and so on.

Advertisements

The following advertisements belong to a tradition of advertising which presents the product in a fairly direct and open way, drawing attention to its special features. Consider the television advertisement scripts on pages 108–9 and answer the questions below.

The pictures which accompany these advertisements are very persuasive: the people in them are healthy, glowing, and attractive. The product is successful for them. But the words also persuade us this is so.

- Take a highlighter pen and mark the words which are deliberately chosen to appeal to the viewer's good taste.
- What is distinctive about the language of each advertisement?
- On what basis does each advertisement recommend the product?
- Who do you suppose is the intended audience?
- In what way is the language specially chosen to appeal to that audience?

Most people underestimate the power of words on television, because they are so preoccupied with the pictures. The moving image steals attention and viewers forget the powerful and almost subliminal impact of the words.

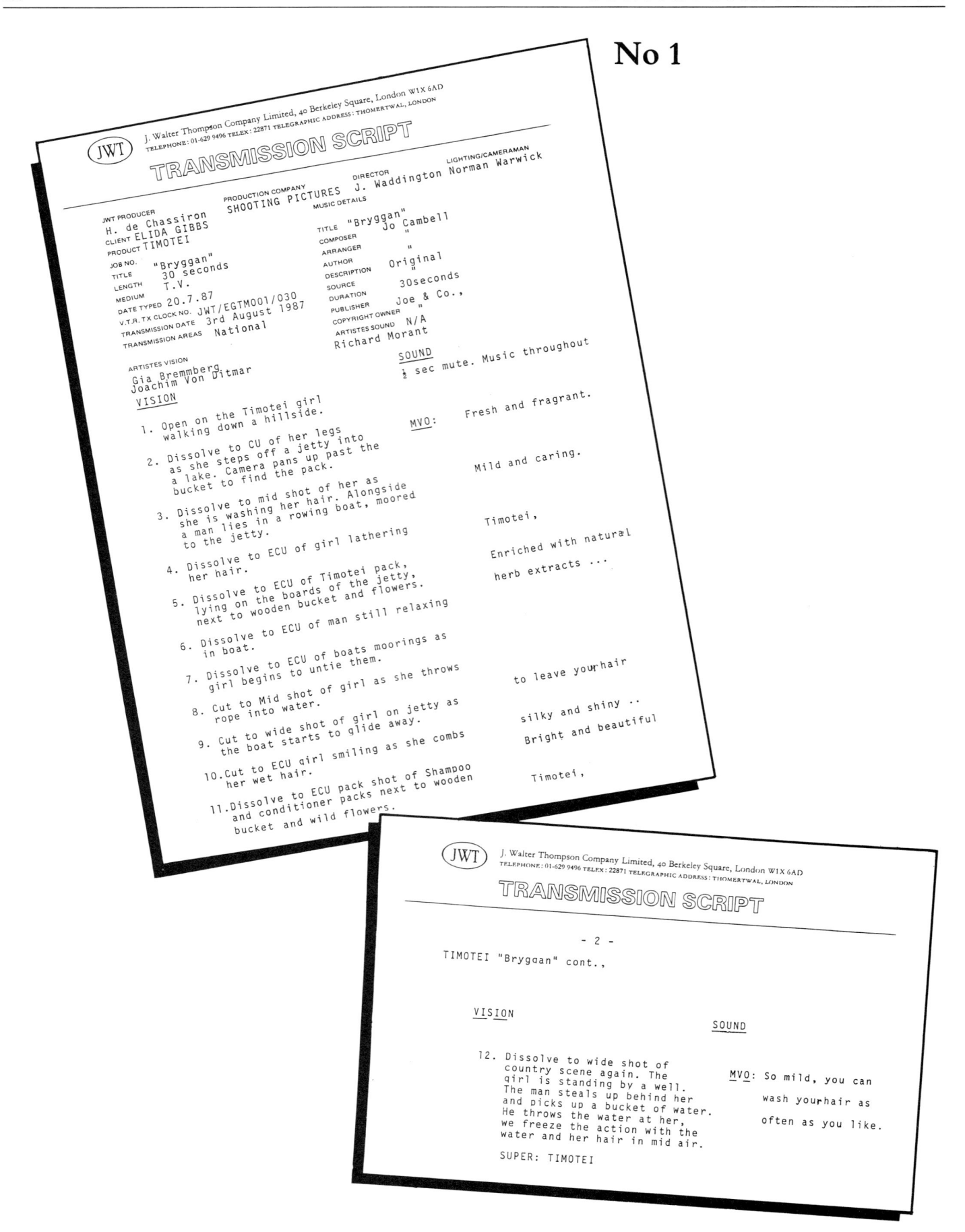

No 1

J. Walter Thompson Company Limited, 40 Berkeley Square, London W1X 6AD
TELEPHONE: 01-629 9496 TELEX: 22871 TELEGRAPHIC ADDRESS: THOMERTWAL, LONDON

TRANSMISSION SCRIPT

PRODUCTION COMPANY	SHOOTING PICTURES
DIRECTOR	J. Waddington
LIGHTING/CAMERAMAN	Norman Warwick
JWT PRODUCER	H. de Chassiron
CLIENT	ELIDA GIBBS
PRODUCT	TIMOTEI
JOB NO.	
TITLE	"Bryggan"
LENGTH	30 seconds
MEDIUM	T.V.
DATE TYPED	20.7.87
V.T.R. TX CLOCK NO.	JWT/EGTM001/030
TRANSMISSION DATE	3rd August 1987
TRANSMISSION AREAS	National

MUSIC DETAILS
- TITLE: "Bryggan"
- COMPOSER: Jo Cambell
- ARRANGER: "
- AUTHOR: "
- DESCRIPTION: Original
- SOURCE: "
- DURATION: 30seconds
- PUBLISHER: Joe & Co.,
- COPYRIGHT OWNER: "
- ARTISTES SOUND: N/A

Richard Morant

ARTISTES VISION
Gia Bremmberg
Joachim Von Ditmar

VISION	SOUND
	½ sec mute. Music throughout
1. Open on the Timotei girl walking down a hillside.	MVO: Fresh and fragrant.
2. Dissolve to CU of her legs as she steps off a jetty into a lake. Camera pans up past the bucket to find the pack.	Mild and caring.
3. Dissolve to mid shot of her as she is washing her hair. Alongside a man lies in a rowing boat, moored to the jetty.	Timotei,
4. Dissolve to ECU of girl lathering her hair.	Enriched with natural herb extracts ...
5. Dissolve to ECU of Timotei pack, lying on the boards of the jetty, next to wooden bucket and flowers.	
6. Dissolve to ECU of man still relaxing in boat.	
7. Dissolve to ECU of boats moorings as girl begins to untie them.	to leave your hair
8. Cut to Mid shot of girl as she throws rope into water.	silky and shiny ..
9. Cut to wide shot of girl on jetty as the boat starts to glide away.	Bright and beautiful
10. Cut to ECU girl smiling as she combs her wet hair.	Timotei,
11. Dissolve to ECU pack shot of Shampoo and conditioner packs next to wooden bucket and wild flowers.	

J. Walter Thompson Company Limited, 40 Berkeley Square, London W1X 6AD
TELEPHONE: 01-629 9496 TELEX: 22871 TELEGRAPHIC ADDRESS: THOMERTWAL, LONDON

TRANSMISSION SCRIPT

- 2 -

TIMOTEI "Bryggan" cont.,

VISION	SOUND
12. Dissolve to wide shot of country scene again. The girl is standing by a well. The man steals up behind her and picks up a bucket of water. He throws the water at her, we freeze the action with the water and her hair in mid air. SUPER: TIMOTEI	MVO: So mild, you can wash your hair as often as you like.

SCRIPT

Client VAN DEN BERGHS **Product** LATTA **Medium** TV
Title FISHING BOAT **Job No.** **Draft No.** 14
Length 40 SECS **Date typed** 16/9/87 **ITCA Submitted/Approved**
Approved: Creative Director [signature] **Account Director** **Client**

VISION

We open on man lazily swimming in water.

He hears the distant chugging of a fishing boat.

Waves ride over man.

Man turns to see old fishing boat coming towards him. On seeing boat he gives a wry smile that says: I'll give you a good run for your money.

Cut to old fishing boat cutting through water.

Cut to man really pounding away.

Cuts to fishing boat and man. It's neck and neck.

Cut to close-up of man's legs, arms and back. His muscles are really pumping away. His legs kicking vigourously.

Cut to close-up of wooden bow. Close-up of water and sea-spray.

Cut to man smiling confidently.

Cut to man swimming past sun.

SOUND

SFX: ENGINE NOISES AND MAN'S BREATHING THROUGHOUT.

MVO: IF YOU LIKE TO KEEP IN THE SWIM, THERE'S A NEW LOW-FAT SPREAD YOU SHOULD GO AFTER.

IT CONTAINS HALF THE FAT OF BUTTER OR MARGARINE.

AND IT'S MADE WITH PURE SUNFLOWER OIL, SO IT'S LOWER IN SATURATES.

SCRIPT

Client VAN DEN BERGHS **Product** LATTA **Medium** TV
Title FISHING BOAT **Job No.** **Draft No.** 14
Length 40 SECS **Date typed** 16/9/87 **ITCA Submitted/Approved**
Approved: Creative Director **Account Director** **Client**

...2/

VISION

Cut to engine straining.

Close-up of man swimming towards camera.

Cut to man walking out of the sea and looking back at boat which carries on. He smiles.

Cut to pack-shot.

Super: For people with an appetite for life.

SOUND

THE NAME OF THIS DELICIOUS NEW SPREAD? LATTA.

No 2

Selling a lifestyle

Not all advertisements describe their products so directly. Where once we were invited to buy for the sake of speed, hygiene, uniqueness, glamour, purity or price, we are now wooed by images of a better lifestyle. The product invites us to share a way of life with the successful, the active, the adventurous and the sophisticated.

Coca-Cola pioneered this kind of advertisement, and it is still going strong. Consider the wording of this example:

The advertisement opens on a shot of a building worker with up-beat music in the background. The picture cuts quickly with the music beat throughout, presenting a stream of shots relating to the lyrics:

Here is another example of an advertisement in the same tradition:

The advertisement opens with a shot of a woman on a balcony at sunrise. She is drinking from a cup. We hear the following song while the picture cuts with the music beat, showing frequent close-ups of the product label:

Get the maximum out of life!
Get the max!
Get the maximum, be your best!
Get the max!
Get the maximum done, get the marks, get the fun!
Maxwell House is the way to the taste of today!
Get the maximum you know how!
Get the max!
Get the Maxwell House, share it out!
Get the max!
Get the maximum taste, get the maximum blend!
Go for maximum pace, get the taste to the end –
Get the max!

Voice-over: GET THE TASTE. GET THE MAX.

THE ART OF PERSUASION

Answer the following questions for each advertisement:

- What direct claims does the advertisement make for the product and its effects?
- What implied claims does it make?
- On what basis does the advertisement recommend the product?
- Who do you suppose is the intended audience?
- In what way is the language specially chosen to appeal to that audience?

The guessing game

Today a new breed of advertisements appeals to an audience which has grown up with television and which has become sophisticated and skilled at viewing. Witty and entertaining, these advertisements draw the viewer into a guessing game about the product.

Consider the wording of the advertisements below and on the next two pages.

No 1

```
SCRIPT
         CLIENT      NATIONWIDE ANGLIA
        PRODUCT      FLEXACCOUNT                        LEAGAS
     DATE TYPED      30.09.87                           DELANEY
          TITLE      INVEST
         REF NO      1838C (R10) Version 1
             TV      X
         CINEMA
          RADIO
         LENGTH      40"
ITCA SUBMITTED
ITCA APPROVED

Open on imposing office. Two little old ladies face a young
official and an old official. (Throughout the commercial the
officials are the epitome of politeness and courtesy).

MARIE             : YES, MY SISTER WANTS TO KNOW WHAT THEY DO WITH
                    THE MONEY IN OUR CURRENT ACCOUNT.
EDWINA            : YES...
SENIOR OFFICIAL   : YES WE INVEST IT
JUNIOR OFFICIAL   : WE INVEST IT MISS JESSOP (ECHOING)
MARIE             : THEY INVEST IT (TO SISTER)
EDWINA            : YES
JUNIOR OFFICIAL   : YES, MISS JESSOP
EDWINA            : YES
MARIE             : YES, THEY INVEST THIS MONEY?
EDWINA            : YES
SENIOR OFFICIAL   : YES, THE MONEY MADE ON THIS MONEY -
MARIE             : THIS MONEY?
EDWINA            : YES
SENIOR OFFICIAL   : THIS MONEY -
MARIE             : THIS MONEY -
SENIOR OFFICIAL   : THIS MONEY -
JUNIOR OFFICIAL   : IS OUR MONEY


SENIOR OFFICIAL   : YES
JUNIOR OFFICIAL   : YES
MARIE             : YES
EDWINA            : THIS MONEY IS YOUR MONEY?
SENIOR OFFICIAL   : YES
EDWINA            : MISS JESSOP, THIS MONEY IS YOUR MONEY
JUNIOR OFFICIAL   : YES
SENIOR OFFICIAL   : THE MONEY MADE ON YOUR MONEY IS OUR MONEY
JUNIOR OFFICIAL   : YES
EDWINA            : YES
MARIE             : THE MONEY MADE ON OUR MONEY....IS YOUR MONEY?
SENIOR OFFICIAL   : YES
JUNIOR OFFICIAL   : YES
SENIOR OFFICIAL   : OH YES
EDWINA            : YES
MARIE             : YES
JUNIOR OFFICIAL   : YES
MARIE             : YES
SENIOR OFFICIAL   : YES

By this time, all four people are somewhat confused. They all say
yes many times.

MVO               : UNLIKE A BANK'S ORDINARY CURRENT ACCOUNT,
                    NATIONWIDE ANGLIA'S FLEXACCOUNT GIVES YOU
                    INTEREST ON YOUR MONEY.

Cut to a completed FlexAccount cheque. A hand then places a cheque
card on top of it.

V/O               : FLEXACCOUNT FROM NATIONWIDE ANGLIA. WE ALWAYS
                    REMEMBER WHOSE MONEY IT IS.
```

THE LEAGAS DELANEY
PARTNERSHIP LIMITED
233 SHAFTESBURY AVE
LONDON WC2H 8EL
TELEPHONE 01 836 4455

- Act out the script.
- What strikes you about the dialogue?
- What strikes you about the language of the voice-over at the end?
- What impression does the advertisement leave of the bank and its staff?
- Why is the mention of the product so brief and so late?
- What personal qualities are we invited to admire or deplore?
- How does this advertisement recommend the product?

No 2

The advertisement opens on a young man, hands behind his head, thinking. He is lying in his designer bed. We look down on him from the ceiling, but in the course of the advertisement, we circle downwards and come close up to his face. We hear his thoughts:

'Now if I tell Mr Green, when I was in the washroom I overheard Mr Brown telling Mr White that it was Mr Grey who'd condoned Mr Black's decision on Project Orange, then Mr Green would view Mr Black in a very different light ... which will then leave Mr Grey with no alternative but to accept the job in the Reykjavik sub-office ... and I'll get his new Vauxhall Carlton CD.'

The picture changes to a shot of the car speeding along with pop music in the background. We hear a voice-over, and the words appear in print:

THE CARLTON FROM VAUXHALL. ONCE DRIVEN, FOREVER SMITTEN.

- In pairs, read the advertisement aloud: young man and 'voice-over'.
- How does the advertisement get the viewer to pay attention?
- What do we learn about the man's work and ambitions?
- Where else would we commonly find language like that in the man's thoughts?
- What personal qualities are we invited to admire?
- Who do you think is the intended audience of this advertisement?
- Most cars in this price bracket are bought by companies as fleet cars. What light does this shed on the advertisement for you?

No 3

There is only one shot in this advertisement: the hands of two men on a restaurant table top, close by their coffee cups. We never see their faces, so their hands provide the only movement in the picture.

FIRST MAN:	Come on, it'll be good.
SECOND MAN:	No it won't.
FIRST MAN:	It will.
SECOND MAN:	It won't.
FIRST MAN:	It will.
SECOND MAN:	*She'll* be there.
FIRST MAN:	Who?
SECOND MAN:	Joyce Oliphant.
FIRST MAN:	Joyce Oliphant? *(laughing)* She won't be there.
SECOND MAN:	She will.
FIRST MAN:	She's probably forgotten all about it by now.
SECOND MAN:	She won't! I know she won't.

THE ART OF PERSUASION

> FIRST MAN: Look, look, look, she won't be there.
> SECOND MAN: Look, I'm *not* going, okay?
> FIRST MAN: You can drive. (*Dangles car keys across table*)
> SECOND MAN: What? Your Cavalier SRi?
> FIRST MAN: Yeah.
> SECOND MAN: Okay, let's go. (*They get up*)
> FIRST MAN: Yeah.
>
> *The picture changes to a shot of the car speeding along with pop music in the background. We hear a voice-over, and the words appear in print:*
>
> THE CAVALIER SRi FROM VAUXHALL. ONCE DRIVEN, FOREVER SMITTEN.

- In pairs, read the advertisement aloud.
- In what ways does the advertisement stimulate the viewer's curiosity?
- What is the role of the car in this scenario?
- What impression do you have of the two men?
- Why are we inclined to trust their opinion of the car?

The subtlety of these advertisements is impressive. They are funny, witty and thought provoking. Nonetheless, there are clear messages in this new generation of advertisements, however subtle they may be. They promote lifestyles which many viewers cannot hope for, and invite us to admire cunning, self-interest, and the acquisition of status symbols. However, it is important to remember that viewers accept the persuasive intent of advertisements, realising that they offer a kind of fantasy world. More suspect, perhaps, are the programmes that follow them, because viewers' defences are down: we're not expecting subtle forms of persuasion then.

The language of programmes

Study the language of these programme extracts and consider what values they promote:

An extract from a business programme

> PRESENTER: UK companies are planning a sharp increase in their capital investments this year, according to a survey published today by the CBI. The quarterly Industrial Trends Survey reports that 28% of firms expect to increase their capital expenditure on buildings in the next 12 months against 22% who don't – that's an overall balance of 6%. Well, Bill Martin's in the Stock Exchange...
> Bill, presumably the fact that they're all prepared or so many of them are prepared to invest so much means they must be **very optimistic about the future**?

BILL: Well, they are optimistic; they've had a very sharp rate of increase in output and capacity constraints now are very, very acute. The amount of spare capacity in the manufacturing sector has never been lower than this according to records, and therefore it's hardly surprising that they are going in for an investment boom, and for the medium term that is welcome news.

PRESENTER: If it's welcome news in the medium term, is it unwelcome for the long-term then?

BILL: For the long-term, I think it is also welcome. We need to see more investment in the manufacturing sector, an increase in the capital base. What concerns me is if the investment boom also goes along with a consumer boom, we will see **too much domestic demand in the British economy**, and that spells trouble for the balance of payments.

- Describe the language used in the extract.
- What assumptions are made about the viewer?
- Discuss the meaning of the emboldened phrases. What other ways are there of expressing these ideas, and why aren't they used?
- What values and institutions are implicitly supported by the language of the programme?

An extract from a soap opera

A young man is sharing a sofa with a much older woman.

WOMAN: Sit down. I want you to take over the Rockstone portfolio – this part of it. I want to put you in charge of all the buying and selling. You get the lot. I give you what you need. Whatever it takes.

MAN: Mrs Rockstone, I . . . er . . . I don't think you're talking to the right guy.

WOMAN: Oh, I think I am.

MAN: Now listen, I don't want this. No way. I've had my bellyful of responsibility. I'm no stockbroker. I've no idea how to analyse earning potential.

WOMAN: What you don't know you'll pick up. You'll do just fine.

MAN: If I were smart, I'd walk out that door and never look back.

WOMAN: But you're not going to. You've never turned your back on a challenge before.

- Compare the business discussion in this extract with that in the previous extract.
- What assumptions are made about the viewer?
- What factors are seen to be central to business success in this extract, and how do they compare with those implied in the previous extract?
- What values and institutions are implicitly supported by the language of the programme?

Special Project: School for Sale

The object of the exercise

This is a day-long practical activity. The object is to commission, plan and produce three contrasting videos of about 3 minutes each, introducing your school or college to three different audiences:

1. *To prospective parents*, persuading them to send their children to the school, emphasising the school's most appealing and successful aspects.

2. *To new students*, giving an insider's guide to the school. The video should present a humorous and candid look at the school and its institutions.

3. *To the school governors*, outlining the changes and improvements students would like to see in the school, its buildings and activities.

Aims

1. To gain an inside understanding of how images can be selected, arranged and presented to give a particular impression.

2. To appreciate the way programmes are tailored to appeal to different audiences.

3. To gain an insight into the roles of the client, advertising agency and television production company in making an advertisement.

4. To gain confidence from experience in:
   - operating video equipment
   - working to specifications
   - criticism, negotiation and decision making

Advance preparations

1. Choose a convenient *date* for making the video. Have a fall-back date in case of rain.

2. Find out what video *equipment* is available and book it, along with extra rooms and materials as necessary.

3. Obtain any *permissions* in advance, for example to record particular interviews and events.

On the day

1. *Split into three commissioning groups, A, B and C*, each one tackling a different audience:

   Group A – parents
   Group B – students
   Group C – governors

   Each group should prepare a short brief for the advertising agency outlining in about 50 words what they want the video to do, to whom it should be addressed and in what circumstances it will be screened. (Time: 10 minutes)

2. *Pass the brief on to the next group*, who will act as the advertising agency. This group will now prepare a rough outline of the video, possibly in sketch form, for the approval of the client.

Brainstorm for ideas to include in the video. Jot down a list of images, interviews and scenes you might use, for example:

```
Video for new students - Ideas:

Basic information - where school is,      School life - rules, discipline,
  how many students, age range,             being absent, catching buses home,
  catchment area.                           etc.
Pictures of school, labs, class-          Interviews - older students recall
  rooms, gym, assembly, rural               first impressions.
  studies area, library.                  Staff - head, deputy, year tutors,
Organisation - tutor groups,                nurse, etc.
  compulsory subjects, options.
First day - what happens,
  arranging the timetable, meeting
  new friends and teachers.
```

(Time: 5 minutes)

Prepare an outline of the video, dividing it into 5 or 6 major sections, for example:

```
Video for new students - Outline structure:

Amusing interviews with older            Start of a typical day - pupils
  students (My first day here).            arriving, tutor groups, assembly
Reassuring commentary from                 - explain routine, point out head
  presenter (We all have expec-            and year tutor, listen in to a
  tations, hopes, fears ...).              bit of typical assembly.
Pictures of younger students             Pictures of lessons in progress -
  around school.                           explain about timetable, setting,
Basic facts about school read              compulsory subjects, listen in to
  out over pictures of different           an English lesson and a maths
  areas of school (labs, library,          lesson.
  etc.).
```

(Time: 15 minutes)

Now prepare a draft script and basic storyboard for the video. The finer details can be settled later, but a key element at this stage of preparation is deciding how to present the material: Will it be documentary style, with a voice-over? Will there be a 'reporter' speaking to camera? Will there be music, interviews or captions, for example:

Presenter to camera:

'Starting a new school is a big moment in anyone's life. It means a new place, new teachers, new friends and new subjects. It can seem like a daunting experience. It's worth remembering that everyone in school has been through this same experience, and whilst you will inevitably have worries, you'll soon find lots of things to enjoy about it.'

(Time: 45 minutes)

3 *Return the material with a spokesperson to the client commissioning group.* The commissioning group should now consider its reaction to the material prepared by the advertising agency:

- Is it suitable for the intended audience?
- Does it cover everything you would wish?
- Do you wish to add, change or delete any elements of the video? (Time: 10 minutes)

4 *Pass the material back to the advertising agency, along with any necessary amendments.* This group should now refine the plan, taking account of the client's comments, to produce a storyboard with sufficient detail for the production company to use it to shoot the video. (Time: 30 minutes)

5 *Pass the storyboard on to the final group,* who will act as the television production company that actually shoots the video. This group should check that the plan given to them by the advertising agency seems feasible. Minor adjustments will probably be necessary.

When the production group is satisfied that any major problem areas have been resolved, collect the video equipment and prepare a signing-out list, so that the teacher will know who is where at any particular moment. Always sign out before you leave the classroom. Consider the video one section at a time.

Rehearse and record the first section. Advice about the allocation of jobs and recording techniques can be found in the section entitled *Try It Yourself* on page 128. At this stage you may find it necessary to modify your plans. Allowances should be made for problems and opportunities which arise in rehearsal. If a scene does not work within two takes, rethink your approach, and try to keep to your schedule.

Move on to the next section. Rotate jobs between sections so that everyone experiences a variety of roles.
(Time: 2½ hours)

Afterwards

In your production group, watch the video you have shot and share your immediate reactions to it. (Time: 15 minutes)

For homework

Write an account of your activities during the day and say what you found interesting, surprising and frustrating about the experience.

Review your own attitude towards the exercise and what you may have learnt from it.

On reflection, what might you do differently another time?

Next lesson

Present your video to the other two groups – the original client and the advertising agency – for their reactions. After watching all three videos discuss the following points:

- How well each video meets the requirements of the original brief.
- The contrast in approach, content and style of the three videos.
- The role of the commentary, particularly where the videos use similar images.
- The appropriateness of each video for its intended audience.
- The relative importance of the client, agency and production groups in shaping the final result.
- How far the medium itself – the camerawork, performance, technical equipment – enables or obstructs the intention of the programme makers.
- Do any of the videos represent the 'truth' about the school? In what sense is there a 'true' view of the school?

Later

Show your videos to their intended audiences. Your teacher will suggest the best person to help you with the arrangements.

Arrange for feedback from the audiences. Their immediate reactions to the video and the questions they ask will suggest how effective it has been. More formal feedback – a questionnaire, for example – may be useful if you want to take the video further. If the video for new students proves successful it could be expanded and refined for use with next year's intake.

PART FOUR
A Point of View

Making a Video in the Community

The biggest problem about making your own video is finding the equipment and skills to do the job. Though most of the population have television sets at home, and are familiar with many types of programme, very few people make television programmes of their own. Here are two cases in which groups learn to make their own videos to publicise a point of view:

Case 1: Improving the Community School pool

In Edinburgh, the Craigroyston Adult Student Association decides to make a video to voice concern about the poor changing facilities at the community school swimming pool. Video equipment is expensive and help is needed initially to set it up and operate the controls. So the first and major problem is finding the equipment and the skills. Community video organisations exist to provide them. It's not their aim to make the video for the group, but to enable them to do it for themselves.

In the first instance, the role of the community video worker is to ask pertinent questions and to direct attention to potential problem areas. Because the number of people involved is small and the issues are local, it is possible to involve everyone and take account of their opinion. In this sense, community video can be more democratic than broadcast television.

With the help of the community video worker, members of the group take the camera into the changing-rooms to record the cramped changing area, the peeling paint and the unsatisfactory layout of the cubicles.

A POINT OF VIEW

After recording the shots, they can begin the painstaking task of editing them together to make the video. The team proceeds shot by shot, experimenting with the order and duration of the pictures until they build up a sequence that conveys the right impression.

Within three weeks, the video is ready to show to the Adult Student Association which requested it, and members are able to express their reactions and make suggestions for improvement. At the same time, discussions begin about screening the video to outsiders. Who should see it and what effect will it have?

Case 2: Facilities for Disabled People

Meanwhile, the Glasgow Film and Video Workshop is helping a group of handicapped people to illustrate their case for improved facilities for people in wheelchairs. Things which are quite straightforward for a walking person can pose aggravating problems for someone in a wheelchair: a spring door, a cluttered passageway, a toilet too cramped to manoeuvre past the door.

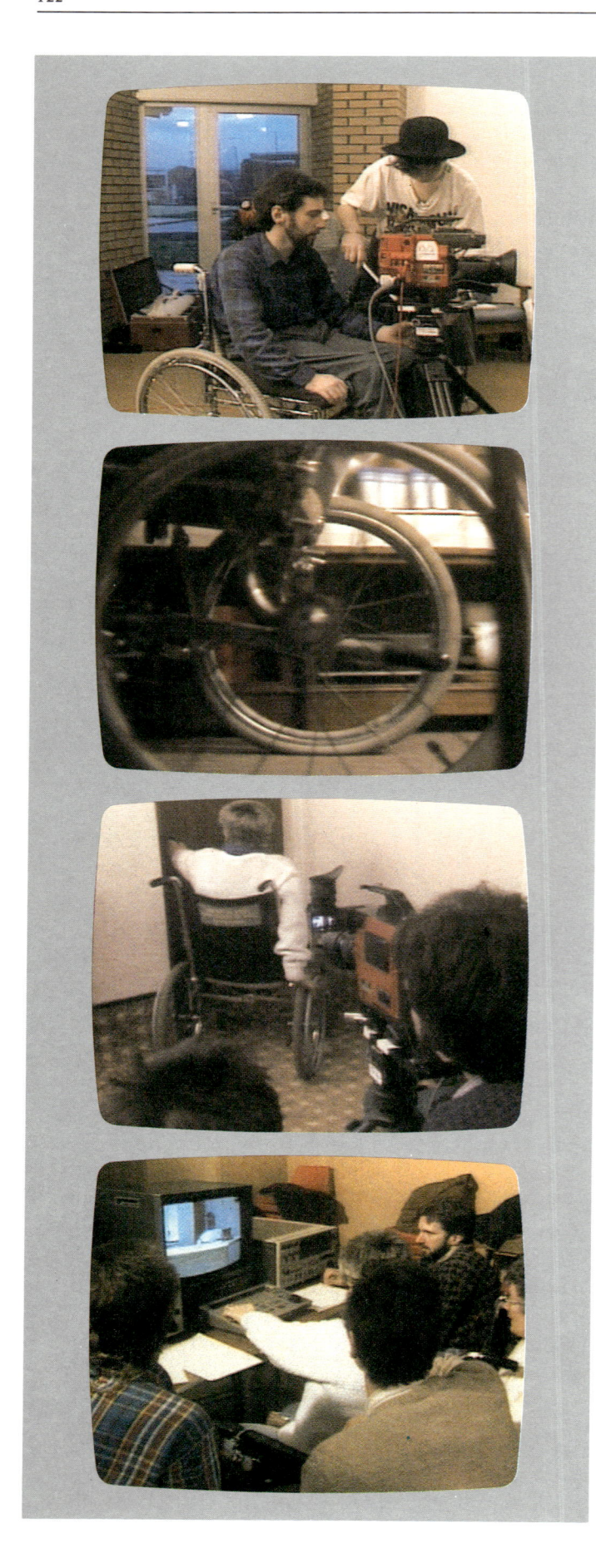

Ironically, the Workshop members also discover that the video equipment is not perfectly designed for people in wheelchairs. Handles get in the way, requiring the user to crane forwards to the viewfinder.

Video can put you in other people's shoes. The camera stoops to floor level to watch the wheelchair snagging on the cluttered furniture.

It follows at shoulder height a woman in a wheelchair straining forwards to push open a spring door. Video can, quite literally, give a new perspective on familiar things.

The Workshop members assist in the editing, using their expertise to help the group gain experience of video for themselves. One of the chief advantages of community video is that the programme is your own. The planning decisions, script, recorded shots and packaging are chosen by you. It would be easy for the experienced staff to make an expert production on the group's behalf, but that would miss the point of community video, which is to open up the medium to people who have need of it, and to help them get the best from it.

Taming the Medium

Dealing with technology

For some, the technology of video can be daunting. The equipment is unfamiliar and unfriendly, and makes them feel clumsy and inept. No one expects to be perfect the first time they attempt something new, but most people do worry about looking foolish.

- Recall the first time you mastered equipment such as riding a bicycle, using a computer, or working a video recorder.
- Discuss ways you found of dealing with the problems. Perhaps you split the task into smaller parts, or identified the main difficulty and concentrated on that?

Fear of technology is a familiar feeling, especially among girls. Boys are expected to be practical and mechanically-minded, while girls have traditionally been brought up with low expectations of their mechanical and technical abilities. But don't be intimidated: the video equipment doesn't know what sex you are. Don't say, 'I could never do that'. You can.

- In groups, set out all the video equipment on a table.
- Work out what each major piece of equipment does and what it is called.
- Have a close look at the video camera. Work out what each bit of it does. Draw a labelled diagram.
- Look at the other pieces of equipment, and draw a diagram which gives their names and shows where all the leads go. Learn how to connect the leads, load the tape, and work the switches.
- Let each person use the camera to look around, record some pictures and experiment with the zoom and focus. Look back at the pictures you have taken.

Camera shyness

Appearing in videos is exciting and, at first, intimidating. Most of us are camera shy to some extent. We know we will never be as slick as the presenters we see on the screen. More than that, we expect we are just too plain, tongue-tied and brainless to do the job. Oddly enough, it is often the most under-confident people who get the most from video work. They are pleasantly surprised to see a respectable performance on the screen. It is important that the working group is sensitive to such shyness and is supportive.

Find out which members of your group are going to find video appearances trying, and consider how they might accomplish their performance with minimum anxiety.

Here are some ideas to help reluctant performers:

- use a mask
- read from cue cards
- shoot interviews over the shoulder or sideways, not face on
- rehearse
- re-record
- allow extra time
- choose active parts which leave little time for self-consciousness

Some people feel vulnerable because they have no control over the image that appears on the screen. Women feel particularly self-conscious, having to live up to an 'ideal' image of the slim and sophisticated woman which is promoted daily in the media. The exercises which follow are designed to help you to overcome camera shyness. Their purpose is not to push you through an embarrassing ordeal, but to help you overcome your shyness and take control of your screen image – to use the camera much as you would use a pen to write about yourself. If you are desperately anxious, do the exercises yourself, but if you can place your trust in a small number of friends, follow the exercises in a group. It is less hassle if someone else operates the camera under your instruction.

Exercise 1

Sit on a chair in front of the camera to reveal you waist upwards (newscaster distance), and place the monitor where you will be able to see yourself on screen. Look at the screen, not at the camera.

Make these faces:

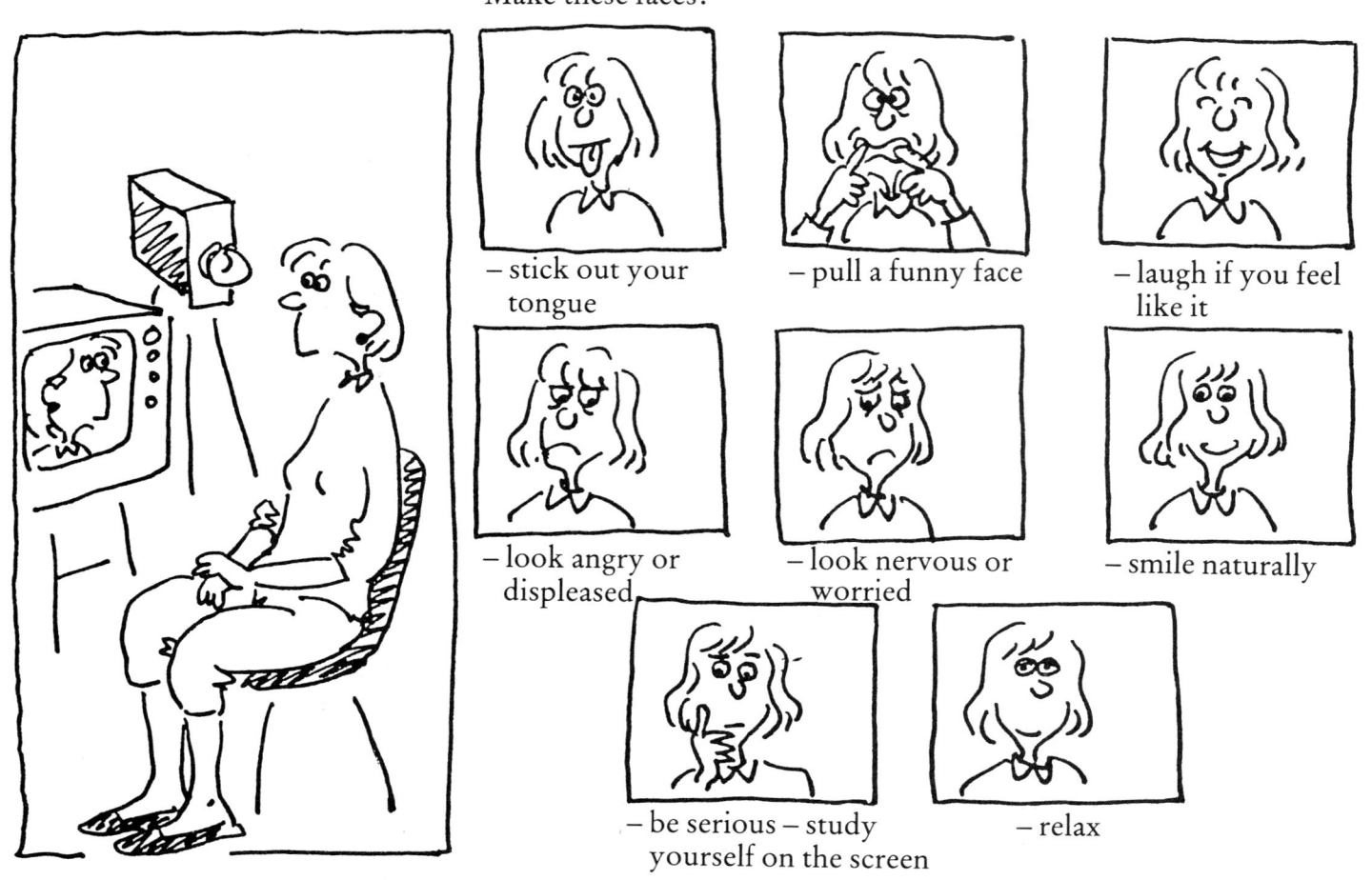

- stick out your tongue
- pull a funny face
- laugh if you feel like it
- look angry or displeased
- look nervous or worried
- smile naturally
- be serious – study yourself on the screen
- relax

A POINT OF VIEW

- What did you find interesting or disturbing about this exercise?
- Re-frame the camera onto your face only. Try out the faces again.
- Did you react differently to them this time?

Exercise 2

Stand up and allow the camera to show your head and shoulders.
Now move the camera to see yourself from the side.
Now move it so it looks down on you.
Now move it so it looks up to you.

- What effect does the position of the camera have on you and the way you appear on screen?

Exercise 3

Put the camera in one corner of the room and walk towards the monitor. It is easy if there is a camera operator to follow your movements. If you are working alone, put the camera close to the monitor so it keeps your face in vision for as long as possible.

Watch yourself
- walking
- approaching a chair and sitting down
- simply standing

- Apart from being self-conscious, is there anything you notice about your own stance and gestures? It can be useful to see yourself as others see you.

Exercise 4

Imagine you have arrived for an interview or to meet your boy or girl friend's Mum for the first time. If you are working in a group, then someone can play this scene with you. Record the scene so that you can see it later, rather than having to look over a shoulder at the monitor.

Walk up to the other person, shake hands as you say hello, and accept an invitation to sit down. Start a conversation. There's no need to continue further than one or two exchanges.

It may come easily to you to 'act natural, be yourself', but most of us need to build up confidence. Take time to rehearse the exercise until you find a way of doing it which looks and feels comfortable. Afterwards, review your performance on the tape.

Exercise 5

Read through this passage until it is familiar:

> Today 5 people were injured – not because of their own foolishness, but because of someone else's mistake. The police have officially called it 'an accident' but there are many people who would call it sabotage.

Read it in front of a camera in the following ways:

1. Standing across the room, behind a desk, as a political leader would speak to a mass meeting.
2. Sitting at a desk, reading the script as a newscaster.

3 Speaking down to your slave or servant.
4 Sitting comfortably having an interesting discussion at a friend's house.

Do this exercise if you have someone else available to operate the camera.

Exercise 6

- What differences do you notice in your reading and the way you behave as you speak?

Sit down and make yourself comfortable.
Read the speech from Exercise 5.
Ask your camera operator to vary the camerawork each time:

First reading: Start with the head and shoulders and gradually zoom in on the eyes.
Second reading: Show a close-up of the hands only.
Third reading: Slowly circle around.
Fourth reading: View from the side. But at the second sentence, the speaker turns to look directly into the camera.

- Review the results and assess the impact of the camerawork in each case. How does the camerawork affect the meaning of the script?

Exercise 7

You won't need a camera for this exercise.

1 During the day, imagine there is a camera focused on you in 30 second bursts. You may be walking along, talking, eating, sitting in a class. Think of a context. For example, you may be appearing in a play or a documentary.

- How does the imaginary camera affect your behaviour?
- What light does it cast on the things going on around you?
- What is different when you mentally 'stop' the imaginary camera?

2 Next, try taking mental snapshots of scenes throughout the day. Frame the picture by creating a square with your fingers and take a mental snap by blinking. When you get used to this, you can dispense with the fingers and the blinking. This is actually quite a useful skill for composing photographs.

3 Next, try taking mental videos of scenes around you.

- What is the effect of seeing scenes through a mental camera?

Don't get hooked on this exercise. Use it sparingly once you've got the point. It can sometimes put events in a fresh light for you, but not if you are persistently detached from your surroundings because of it.

On television, everything has a context. People do things because the plot is leading somewhere. Events are shown on the news because they are of national importance. Scenes are recorded because the programme has a point to make about them. But your own life is not like this. It is not a play or a news story or a documentary. It is neither scripted nor edited. The meaning of the events in your life is for you to decide.

If you appear on video, or if you are asked one day to appear on television, it is important that you have control of the meanings it makes. Television has the power to present almost any deed in almost any way. If you want to be seen on your own terms, make sure you have control over what is shown.

Ask yourself and the programme maker:

Exactly *what* will be shown?
How, *when*, and *to whom* will it be shown?
Can you see a *script* or a list of questions in advance?
Can you *check it* after it's been edited?
Can you *stop it* being shown?

Try it Yourself

Making your own video is rewarding and challenging. If you have not done it before, you may not know where to begin. This section will help to get you started. It doesn't matter that you have no hands-on experience right now; that is something you will pick up on the way. Like learning to ride a bike, you will discover the best way to do it as you go along.

Don't be put off

Television offers us glossy expert videos: everyone knows what professional camerawork looks like, and it's easy to be disappointed with your own first efforts, by comparison. Don't be; you'll soon get the idea. You can use broadcast television to provide clues about how to shoot your video, without trying to copy its appearance. It's best to work in a group, sharing ideas and responsibilities. Don't expect to get everything right first time. It's a process of trial and error.

Finding an idea

You can use video for fun, recording people and events close to you. You can also use it to make a point. Many community groups use video to illustrate their campaigns because it is such a striking visual medium.

Think of *two* subjects for video recordings lasting under two minutes each. Don't choose anything too ambitious to start with. Just something that interests you and would be fun to do, for example,

- a comic sketch
- the state of the bike sheds
- an interview

Allocating roles

Making a video is a team effort. This is true also of the programmes you see on television. One of the problems you will face is working together in a group. It is all too easy for the enthusiasts to take over, and the rest drop out. It is more interesting if jobs are shared around. Discuss what jobs need to be done.

- Make a list of the job titles which appear in the credits at the end of a television programme and discuss what these jobs might involve.

A POINT OF VIEW

You won't need all these personnel for your own video. Decide which ones you do need, and choose which person in the group will do each task. Some people will have to double up, and everyone must chip in with ideas and advice.

Planning ahead

1. Choose *one* of your video ideas to start off with. Discuss what you are going to do and where you will shoot it.
2. Decide what *equipment* you will need to shoot the video.
3. Discuss what *costumes* and *props* you will need.
4. Choose a location with adequate *light*. Video cameras do not work well in dull indoor conditions. Get advice from someone with previous experience of recording indoors.
5. Obtain any necessary *permission* to record in particular places.
6. Allow *time* for re-recording scenes that need several 'takes'.
7. Write an outline or *script*. Work out what each shot will look like – you will find it useful to prepare a *storyboard* like the one shown below.
8. Have a *rehearsal* without cameras.
9. Draw up a *timetable* of events.

A storyboard is a cartoon version of the video which helps in the planning stage. Here's an example, drawn up by Tony Lavender of Jourdanhill College of Education.

Pictures **Sound and/or dialogue**

Aircraft noise as it lands *or* music

Airport building noise in background

Dialogue of X greeting Y.
Airport concourse noise low in background

There is a blank storyboard sheet on page 133 for duplication.
You can describe the scene in words if you prefer, but you must give the camera distance and angle. A detailed conversation may require a full script.

Shooting the Scene

When it comes to recording, remember that videotape can be erased, so you can always go back and record over mistakes. To avoid having to remake the whole thing, break the recording up into sections. Then if one section goes wrong, you only have that bit to retake. Periodically, you will have to stop the recording to reposition the camera between shots. It is boring to watch two minutes of the same camera angle, and that is another good reason for repositioning the camera.

It helps if you know what the various camera moves are called. Here is an abbreviated glossary:

Pan – a horizontal movement of the camera – from right to left or left to right – while the camera mounting stays fixed.

Tilt – a vertical movement of the camera – up or down – while the camera mounting stays fixed.

Track – the camera and its mounting moves towards or away from the scene.

Zoom – the camera mounting stays fixed, while the zoom control changes the focal length of the lens, for example from a close up – zoomed *in* – to a wide angle – zoomed *out*.

The distance of the camera is described as shown in the illustration below left.

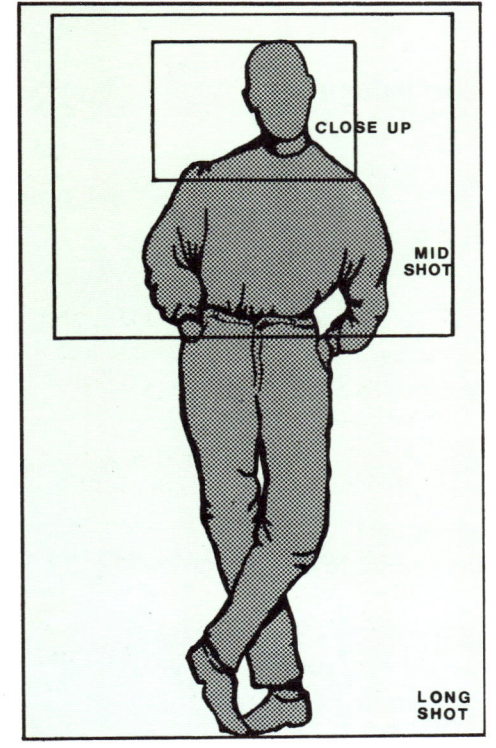

Here, Tony Lavender offers some advice on camera technique: some advice on camera technique:

Composing Pictures

It is important to think initially about each individual shot and then to consider how adjacent shots look together. The following points can be borne in mind:

Balance – arrange images within a frame so they 'balance' properly e.g.:

(a) One person looking at or presenting directly to camera would normally be centred in the frame.

(b) One person looking left (or right) out of frame should have space to look into ('looking room').

(c) Avoid too much or too little space ('headroom') between the top of someone's head and the top of the frame.

(d) Avoid flowers, plants, etc. growing out of/balanced on the top of people's heads.

(e) Adults interviewing children should sit or crouch so that their eye-line matches that of the child.

(f) Avoid excess space between subjects and keep them away from edge of frame.

(g) When a panning shot is covering a moving person, lead that person, do not trail.

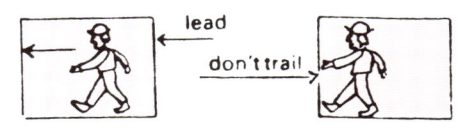

(h) When the same person or object is moving in two successive shots, ensure that the movement is in the same direction.

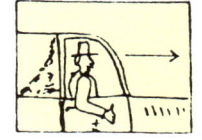

Depth – compose in depth as far as possible

For example, when covering two person interviews or discussions, compose shot over the interviewer's shoulder to improve composition and reduce the gap between people to a minimum.

Bear in mind, too, the lighting and sound requirements:

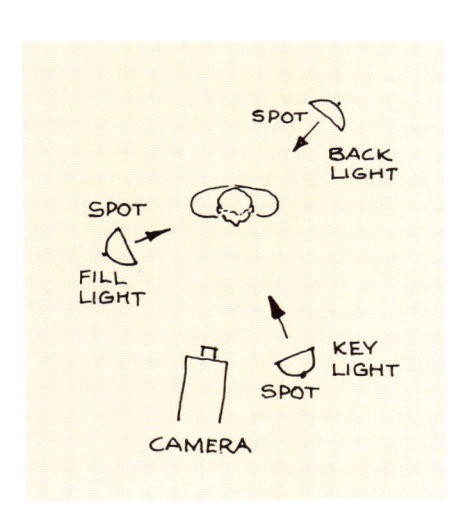

Most simple video cameras are supplied with built-in microphone and a socket for plugging in an extension microphone. The built-in microphone has an all-round (omni-directional) pick up pattern which will record all noises in the locality of the camera. An extension microphone should preferably be used for interviews and discussions with the microphone being placed or held 9 to 12 inches from the sound source.

Three-point lighting gives the best effect for video productions, but often the necessary equipment is not available in educational establishments. Cameras should usually be set up pointing away from the windows of a room, if inside, or with the sun behind the camera if outside. Photographic lights when available can be used as fill or back lights when light from a window source or the sun fills the role of key light.

And finally, some general hints:

DO take a wide angle or long shot of a scene as early as possible to help define the 'geography' of the situation.

Although the close up is the essence of television, DON'T neglect the wide angle or long shot.

DO keep the camera as close to the eye-line of the subject as possible, unless a high or low angle shot is required for some special effect.

DON'T cut between shots which look very similar.

DON'T pan, tilt, zoom, track without adequate motivation.

DON'T over-use a zoom lens.

DO pan with movement, and not over a static scene as far as possible.

DON'T cut between a still shot and a panning shot.

DO bear the problems of lighting in mind.

DON'T forget the sound requirements.

Self-assessment

If this is your first video, don't be a perfectionist. You haven't got the time or the equipment to make videos of broadcast quality. It's more important to have fun and gain confidence. As you look back over your work, discuss the weaknesses, of course, but also look for the good points.

As a group, ask yourselves what impression the video makes. Is it *interesting*? Do you find it easy to *understand*? Does it make any particular *point*? What do you think of the lighting, sound, and overall *technical quality*? Do the joins between shots look and sound smooth? Pick out any obvious *blunders*, and try to pinpoint what is wrong. Look, too, at the *good bits*, and say what it is that makes them work.

Finally, consider the way you felt making the video. What did you find most difficult and most enjoyable? How did it feel to see your work on screen? And what would you improve if you had another go?

STORYBOARD

TITLE _____   NAME _____   DATE _____

LOCATION _____   SEQUENCE _____   PAGE ____ of ____

DIRECTOR _____   SCRIPT _____

PARTICIPANTS _____   CAMERA/VIDEO _____

	PICTURE	ACTION/EFFECTS/PROPS	SOUND/SPEECH
Shot No. .... Time .... Camera			
Shot No. .... Time .... Camera			
Shot No. .... Time .... Camera			
Shot No. .... Time .... Camera			
Shot No. .... Time .... Camera			

Making the Most of It

Working on video is rewarding and can be lots of fun – but it isn't automatically the best medium to choose. It all depends on what you want to do.

In order to identify the strengths and limitations of the video medium, consider the following passages and how you would adapt them for television.

Use a marker pen to highlight those sections which could be easily adapted to video in the form of pictures and dialogue. Mark in another colour those sections which would be more difficult to televise, and indicate how you would deal with them, for example leave them out, add a voice-over, use graphics, employ suggestive music and lighting.

Narrative: A passage from D. H. Lawrence's novel *The Rainbow*

They came out of the café.

'Is there anything you would like to do?' he said.

'Is there anything we *can* do?'

It was a dark, windy night in March.

'There is nothing to do,' she said.

Which was the answer he wanted.

'Let us walk then – where shall we walk?' he asked.

'Shall we go to the river?' she suggested, timidly.

In a moment they were on the tram, going down to Trent Bridge. She was so glad. The thought of walking in the dark, far-reaching water-meadows, beside the full river, transported her. Dark water flowing in silence through the big, restless night made her feel wild.

They crossed the bridge, descended, and went away from the lights. In an instant, in the darkness, he took her hand and they went in silence with subtle feet treading the darkness. The town fumed away on their left, there were strange lights and sounds, the wind rushed against the trees, and under the bridge. They walked close together, powerful in unison. He drew her very close, held her with a subtle, stealthy, powerful passion, as if they had a secret agreement which held good in the profound darkness. The profound darkness was their universe.

Comment: Handling hijackers

The negotiators are skilled in psychology. They cannot give way to hijackers' demands for fear of encouraging further hijacks, but neither can they risk the lives of hostages by rejecting them outright. Largely, they play a waiting game, promising, delaying and containing the situation until tension forces the hijackers to reduce the demands. Their strategy is sensitive to the emotional swings of the hijackers. The pressures are immense for everyone involved. But hijackers are highly committed, and there is always the risk that they will martyr themselves for their cause, taking with them innocent lives. These immediate risks are measured against the long-term risks, as well as the immediate political pressures and military situation.

Demonstration: A recipe for Spicy Vegetable Risotto

Ingredients:
- 1 tbs. oil
- 1 leek
- 1 carrot
- 1 onion
- 100 g mushrooms
- 1 green pepper
- 2 tomatoes
- salt, pepper, cumin and coriander
- half a cup of stock
- 100 g brown rice
- a little chopped parsley

(serves 2)

Chop the vegetables and fry them gently for 3 minutes in a large pan. Add spices to taste. A few cumin and coriander seeds give a fragrant, spicy flavour.

Cook for a further 3 minutes before adding stock. Cover the pan and simmer for 15 minutes. The vegetables should be tender but not mushy.

Meanwhile, cook the rice in plenty of boiling salted water for 30 minutes, then rinse.

Stir the rice into the vegetables and cook them together over a low heat for 5 minutes. Turn the mix into a warm serving bowl and sprinkle with parsley.

Explanation: What makes a car skid

The role of the driver is the first thing to consider in a skid. The car and the road conditions are both of secondary importance. A skid is not something that just happens. Even if the conditions are slippery and icy, a car travelling at a steady speed on a straight and level road is most unlikely to skid. The danger arises when the driver changes speed or direction. In these circumstances, the car needs more grip from the tyres, and if the driver demands more grip than the tyres can give, the car will skid.

So skids are much more likely when a car is accelerating, braking, turning a corner, or travelling up or down a hill.

Description: A landscape

The valley is huge and impressive. From the road above, one can barely pick out the cattle grazing by the river or the people busy about the fields. The town seems remote and tiny, though just an hour ago we passed through its thronging market street. Up here, all is cool and silent and the sky seems larger, immense.

Centuries ago, our guide explains, the valley was gouged out of rock by a glacier from the snowy peak behind us. It spilt over from the scooped hollow on the mountain top and carved its way down the valley to produce this huge, flat-bottomed hollow. When the glacier melted, it deposited its load of rubble and eroded rock on the valley floor to become the pasture soil on which the cows now graze. The river which once owned the valley now picks its way over the flat floor.

- What problems did you encounter in adapting the material for television?
- Outline the various strategies which you employed to get round the problems.
- Consider the suitability of video for these eight subjects:

    – a horse race
    – a complicated piece of legislation about Sunday trading

- what the baby looked like when it was first born
- a weather forecast for shipping
- a play about the life and times of someone famous
- a stand-up comedian
- a political debate
- the state of disrepair in local flats

- Which of the items would be best accomplished on video?
- Could any of them be communicated more effectively in another medium such as a written report, an audio tape recording or a photograph?
- Compare video, writing, photography and audio-recording under these headings:

   - cost
   - ease of use
   - time it takes
   - skills needed
   - equipment needed
   - ease of presentation to an audience
   - good at communicating information
   - good at communicating experience
   - good at communicating thought and feeling
   - good at inviting close study
   - good at presenting everyday events and objects
   - good at reporting immediate action

- What conclusions can you draw about the strengths and limitations of video as a medium?

Purpose, audience and context

In making your own video, you must have a clear idea of its purpose, its intended audience and the context in which it will be viewed. Knowing these things will help you to present the right information at the right time and in the most effective way.

Here is a plan for a video:

> **'Moving Up' – A five-minute video about our local primary school for new pupils**
> *Purpose:* To show prospective pupils what the school is like outside and inside, and to reassure them that school will be interesting and friendly. To give them an impression of what being at school will be like.
> *Audience:* Children in their last year of nursery school.
> *Context:* To be shown as part of a week's activities in the nursery school in preparation for the transfer to primary school. The week will include talks and discussion, a visit from the headteacher and the class teacher, along with some pupils, and finally a visit to the new school.

- Using this information, decide what kind of things should be shown in the video, and what you would leave until later. Discuss what tone you would adopt in your introduction.
- What changes would you make to your plans if the intended audience for the video was the parents of prospective pupils?

- Now prepare plans for *three* videos selected from the following list and present them under the headings:
    - Title and length of video
    - Purpose
    - Audience
    - Context (including when and where it would be screened)
    - List of items to include
    - Other relevant information

1 A video introducing new students to the school *or* fifth year students to the sixth form.
2 The council have made available £500 for a group of young people to undertake a project over the summer which will be 'of benefit to the local community'. Make the case for your project on video.
3 You can't stand the state of the boy's loos/dilapidated huts/bike sheds/desks/noticeboards any longer. Make a video to get something done about it.
4 A video to entertain visitors at Open Day or Parents' Evening.
5 A video to deter students from eating too much unhealthy junk food.

Audience research

Unlike broadcast television, community video has no ready-made audience. One has to be singled out and persuaded to watch. Researching this audience is of prime importance. If you want action on an issue, you have to know whom to approach, where to find them, how to appeal to their better nature, how to address them, when to approach them for the maximum impact, and what arguments they will find most persuasive.

Identify the appropriate audience for videos on these issues:

1 The abuse of local parks by dog owners.

2 Local homelessness.

3 Equipping your local school with facilities for students in wheelchairs.

- Where will you start looking for the appropriate audience?
- What do you need to know about them?
- Who can tell you?
- How will this information influence your video?

At first, using the medium of video to make your case might seem an obvious and straightforward idea. But a good video depends on careful planning. Ask yourself first of all if the issue will lend itself to television. If it will, tailor the video and its commentary to the intended audience. Making your own video may not result in a glossy, professional finish, but it can be much more effective if the issues are local, the purpose is well defined, and the audience is known.

Reclaiming the Image

Images of people

Television is a powerful force in forming opinions and our images of other people. If television gives us a particular impression of foreigners, rich people and teenagers, for example, then it has a responsibility to ensure those images are fair and justifiable. You know yourself how inhibiting it is to be misunderstood or underrated.

- Discuss briefly what impression of the following people we may gain from these television programmes:
    - mothers in advertisements
    - yuppies in dramas
    - middle-aged couples in situation comedies
    - teenagers in soap operas
    - black people in the news

Diane Abbott – often in the news

With any group in society, it is all too easy to create stereotypes. This is not a conspiracy. Comedy relies on stereotypes because people can identify them quickly, while the news deliberately selects events of conflict and significance. In this way, the humdrum details of everyday life – the ordinary human details – are filtered out of television. They don't make for compulsive viewing. 'Slice of Life' documentaries do attempt to deal with this area, but it is difficult to capture the texture of everyday life on video.

- Imagine you are approached by a television station that wishes to make a documentary about 'A day in the life of a teenager in modern Britain'.
- What problems might the team encounter in making this programme over a period of one day?
- How would the presence of the cameras and the crew of technicians affect your behaviour, for example in the classroom or at dinner tonight?
- What research would the production team need to carry out before recording?
- Imagine the programme that may have been made based on your experiences so far today. What would be included and what omitted? How representative of your life would the end product have been?

Self image

Some cultures fear the camera because they feel it 'steals' their image and makes it the property of someone else. It's not a naive fear. All people want to be seen in a fair light. We consider it our right to put a vile passport photograph in the bin, or to exclude a rotten holiday snap from the album. It's a question of defining one's own image.

You have probably attempted autobiography in writing. For example, you may have written about a personal experience for your English teacher, or kept a private diary at home, or used a reading journal in literature lessons. You have almost certainly attempted autobiography already today in the form of discussion, by telling someone else about something that happened to you.

- Working in groups of three or four, recall a recent experience you have had, such as an argument, an embarrassment, or the arrival of a piece of news and your reactions to it. You will have forgotten some of the details, but the overall impression is still there. Ask each of the people in your group to take a part, and organise a camera operator. You can act yourself, or ask someone else to take your part. Describe the incident to the group and get them to re-enact it. Direct them if there are particular words or movements they should make. Rehearse it several times, making adjustments until it feels close to the original event, and then record it.
- What effect did the activity have on your view of the original event?
- What compromises were involved in recreating the event?
- Are the same compromises made if you write or tell a personal experience?

The camera invites us to observe events from its position, so autobiography is a very demanding subject. In our own lives, we never appear in vision, other than in a reflection. Yet memory replays experience as a drama. Over a period of time we select, shape and interpret our experiences. It's hard to know if our memory of an event is accurate.

- Ask other members of the group to recall an experience you shared in the past and notice how each person recalls it in a different way.

The meaning of an experience becomes clearer in the telling. We mull over events, recount them to other people and record them in order to understand our own lives better. Video is neglected as a tool of autobiography, but it does have certain advantages, because it can represent an event to us from another angle, so that we can see it again from the outside.

Making videos for ourselves

Community video exists to allow people to control their own image. It gives them a small opportunity to project their own views for a change. Community video is not a rival to broadcast television; it lacks the equipment, money and mass audience. But it can be important to the people who make it, and it is small and flexible enough for everyone to have their say. Most importantly, it can identify its audience and therefore speak more directly and pertinently to them.

Community video offers great opportunities to people who are normally excluded from broadcast television. It is open to anyone who has the initiative to get on with the job, while broadcast television is virtually closed to people without the 'right' qualifications and attitudes.

Turn on the television set this evening and watch a minute on each channel, noting down the people who appear and their roles.

- How well represented are
    - young people
    - old people
    - working-class people
    - wealthy people
    - black people
- What differences do you notice in the roles of men and women?
- What social background can you assume from the way television presenters dress and speak?
- Account for the trends you identify.

Like all large institutions, television stations tend to be resistant to change. Broadcast television is becoming more representative but change is slow to filter through to the screen. Community video is available now for people who want to make it.

- What are the major differences between broadcast television and community video? Consider:
    - size, and how this might affect programme making
    - finance
    - how decisions are made
    - how jobs are split up and allocated
    - the audience
    - how success is judged

Having a say about broadcast television

Television companies have to respond to viewers. An audience which votes with its feet – or its remote control button – soon has an impact on scheduling because television is dependent on its audience ratings for its money. Poor programmes get dropped when enough people switch over. That is why you must become a selective viewer, choosing what you want to watch and thinking critically about the programmes you see. Whether you talk about your reactions or write reviews, it is worthwhile letting the television stations know. There are a limited number of opportunities to influence them: through letters, video-box appearances, telephone complaints and so on.

- What programmes exist to air viewers' opinions?
- What other ways are there of getting a hearing?

To be an articulate critic, you need to know how television works and how it makes its meanings. General impressions are usually dismissed as a matter of opinion, but it is hard to dismiss precise criticism of specific camera shots and particular words. Making your own video is a good way of gaining an awareness of these techniques, but paying fresh attention to the composition of the programmes on television tonight is equally valuable. You can help better television to emerge by becoming a better 'armchair critic'.

Special Project: Video Dispatch

The object of the exercise

This is a day-long practical activity. The object is to produce a short video message for a real audience with a particular purpose such as:

1 A video drawing the attention of the local council to the state of nearby playground facilities, and suggesting improvements.

2 A video addressed to a class in another country, inviting them to return their own video, and introducing to them the class, the school, and aspects of local life which may be of interest.

3 A video to be sealed in a 'time capsule', to be unearthed in AD 3000, sending greetings to future students and depicting a typical day in the life of the school.

Aims

1 To develop confidence in video as a medium for the expression of one's own perceptions and observations.

2 To appreciate the needs and interests of the audience and to tailor material accordingly.

3 To gain confidence from experience in:
- operating video equipment
- co-operating in teamwork
- taking responsibility and making decisions
- scripting and appearing on video

Advance preparations

1 Choose a convenient *date* for making the video. Have a fall-back date in case of rain.

2 Find out what video *equipment* is available and book it, along with extra rooms and materials as necessary.

3 Obtain any *permissions* in advance, for example to record particular interviews and events.

4 Select an *audience* for your video dispatch.

On the day

1 Collect the *video equipment*.

2 Prepare a *signing-out list*, so that the teacher will know who is where at any particular moment. Always sign out before you leave the classroom.

3 *Get into groups.* A large class with enough equipment may like to split into several groups, each one producing its own dispatch.

4 Discuss the interests and needs of the *audience*. What they will and won't know. The best way to address them. When and where to reach them. What sort of information is relevant to them.

5 *Brainstorm for ideas* to include in the video. For example:

> **Local playground**
>
> St Peter's Park:
> broken swing
> step missing off slide
> peeling paint
> graffiti
> concrete base dangerous
> filthy paddling pool
> dog mess
> litter from ice cream van
>
> BUT
>
> well-kept lawns
> lots of new trees and plants
> popular with families
> 'adventure' equipment very imaginative
> plenty of swings
>
> POINTS TO MAKE
>
> needs evening lock-up
> Spring clean/repaint
> mend dangerous equipment immediately
> needs benches for parents
> soft base in play area (woodchips, rubber)
> waste bins
> poop scoops/dog area
>
> interview Local Councillor – money/safety, etc.
> Jimmy Smiggins (swing accident last week)
> pictures – unsupervised play
> Residents' Association

6 Prepare an *outline* of the video, dividing it into five or six major sections. For example:

(a) Introduction – outline problem
(b) Detailed pictures of equipment
(c) Interview – children, parents, residents
(d) Suggestions for improvements (pictures from successful parks?)
(e) Interview councillor
(f) Conclusion – sum up recommendations

7 Work out a *timetable* for the day's activities, based on your outline. Leave time to view and discuss the video at the end.

8 Prepare a *draft plan* for the first section of your video. This may take the form of a script, a storyboard, a detailed list of interview questions or even a list of particular shots, depending on the task in hand.

A POINT OF VIEW

PLAYGROUND FACILITIES – VIDEO TO COUNCIL

<u>End of school day – local children come out of school</u>

Voice-over: 'It's 3.30, and local primary school pupils leave school and head for home or the swings.'

<u>Playground begins to fill up</u>

'St. Peter's Park is just over the way and many parents and pupils visit the swings on their way home. Up to 30 pupils use these swings between 3.30 and 4.30 each weekday.'

<u>Zoom out to reveal presenter</u>

'As you can see, the playground is popular and convenient. The park itself is very attractive, especially since the new flower beds have bloomed, and the equipment in the playground is modern and imaginative. But is it safe?'

9 *Rehearse and record* the first section. Advice about the allocation of jobs and recording techniques can be found in the section entitled *Try It Yourself* on page 128. You may at this stage find it necessary to modify your plans. Allowances should be made for problems and opportunities which arise in rehearsal. If a scene does not work within two takes, rethink your approach, and try to keep to your schedule.

Move on to the next section. Rotate jobs between sections so that everyone experiences a variety of roles.

Afterwards

Watch your own video and share your immediate reactions to it.

For homework

1 Write an account of your activities during the day and say what you found interesting, surprising and frustrating about the experience.
2 Review your own attitude towards the exercise and what you may have learnt from it.
3 On reflection, what might you do differently another time?

Next lesson

In groups, watch the video again and discuss the following points:

- Which aspects of the video are the most successful – and why?
- How appropriate is each video for its intended audience?
- How far does the medium itself – the camerawork, performance, technical equipment – help or obstruct the intention of the programme makers?

Later

If possible, show your video to its intended audience. Your teacher will suggest the best person to help you with the arrangements. If this is impractical, another class may be a suitable audience.

Arrange for feedback from the audience. Their immediate reactions to the video and the questions they ask will suggest how effective it has been.

Cloze answers

1 genres – types of programme. Soap operas, game shows, documentaries, are all examples of different genres.
2 serial – a serial is an ongoing story in which each episode takes up where the last one left off. Soap operas such as *EastEnders* are serials.
3 episode – a programme that forms part of a series or serial, as opposed to a one-off programme that stands alone.
4 series – a series is made up of episodes which are linked in some way. Unlike a serial, there is no fixed sequence and each can be viewed on its own.
5 resolved – brought to a satisfying conclusion. Audiences expect endings which, if not happy, are just. Even in the saddest of endings, a gleam of hope is seen; someone has grown wiser, perhaps.
6 money
7 love
8 humiliated
9 punished, for example jailed
10 killed
11 sequel – a follow-up episode or series.